Building
a
Biblical
Faith

CW00952263

Building a Biblical Faith

A Seeker's Guide to Christian Theology

Charles H. Bayer

Chalice Press
St. Louis, Missouri

Biblical quotations, unless otherwise noted, are from the *New Revised Standard Version Bible*, copyright 1989, Division of Christian Education of the National Council of the Churches of Christ in the USA. Used by permission.

Cover design: Michael Dominguez

10 9 8 7 6 5 4 3 2 1

Library of Congress Cataloging–in–Publication Data

Bayer, Charles H.
    Building a biblical faith : a seeker's guide to Christian theology / by Charles H. Bayer.
        p.   cm.
    Includes bibliographical references.
    ISBN 0-8272-0220-2
    1. Theology.   2. Bible—Theology.   I. Title.
BR118.B328   1995   94-32750
230—dc20   CIP

Printed in the United States of America

Contents

Dedicated
to all my colleagues
in parish ministry
who take the teaching
of theology seriously.

Preface

The mainline church is in trouble. Nobody needs to make that point these days. We have lost our way, broken loose from our moorings. Not only is the direction gone, but also the passion. We are not certain what we are to be and what we are to do. Answers abound. Books appear by the gross, first viewing with alarm, then analyzing the problem and pointing out possible alternatives. My 1991 book, *Hope for the Mainline Church*, is one of these efforts. What is rarely seen is that when God is about to do a new thing there is often a pause: "silence in heaven for about half an hour." What we view as decay may only be God about to bring to birth something new.

Nevertheless, as I have continued to analyze the multitude of problems facing us, I have concluded that the issue is not sociological or programmatic. It is theological. We have lost our theological roots. Many of those in the pews and some in the pulpits don't understand, have not come to grips with, and cannot articulate what they believe or why. The very word *theology* connotes an abstraction dealt with by those who don't live in the real world, namely theologians who exist in the rarefied air of seminaries. These scholars may talk to each other and write books for each other, but they are out of touch with what is going on in Middletown USA and in the religious lives of the people who live there. So runs the popular wisdom.

The truth is that if layfolk were told what goes on in seminary classes many might be refreshed, liberated, and relieved. Significant numbers have never bought superstition in Christian dress, but haven't known there is an alternative. Nobody has had the courage or seen the need to tell them any different. Or it is assumed that laypeople are not interested in theology, so why bother? Yet for Christians, not to love God with all our minds is to love God only partially.

Consider the role local clergy have assigned themselves, or have assumed by default. A good friend of mine grew up with a father who was the manager of a small retail business. When he entered college, "John" decided to stay as far away from that vocation as possible. Having some religious sensitivities, he selected the ministry for his life's work. John is just a few months from retirement now, and after a lifetime of church work, it has slowly dawned on him that, despite his early intentions, he has spent his life managing a small retail business. He is expected to show a profit, keep the customers happy, have the right products on the shelf, aggressively market, and do all the things a small business person does.

Or we see ourselves as professionals, and expect to be treated as such. At the bottom of the ecclesial heap are pastors of small churches who may just be called "the Minister." In somewhat larger congregations the title is elevated to "the Senior Minister." Among the really tall steeple gang we now have "the Executive Minister."

The typical mainline minister may see himself or herself as the program director of a modest-sized community club. But one finds few clergy these days who see themselves as theologians in residence, or whose main focus is teaching the faith. We are consumed doing other things, and besides, theology is ivory-tower stuff, not down-to-earth stuff. It is difficult to demonstrate that talking about theology has any impact on the really important indexes found in the columns marked "attendance," "additions," or "offerings."

As a result, our congregations may be programmed, entertained, and even cared for, but they are not adequately fed or taught. We have ended up—let us hope the end is not yet—with churches full, or empty as the case may be, of theological and biblical illiterates. The great majority of layfolk have been left either with an understanding of the faith no more mature than the literal interpretation of Bible stories they once heard in Sunday school, or with a theology drawn from whatever fundamentalist author or TV program they happen to catch. Being enamored with our need for young families, we often force new Christians into positions of leadership before they are theologically grounded.

The broad assumption, even among mainline parishioners, is that Pat Robertson has it right. What other models are there? Is it any wonder that in most mainline denominations there seems to be a considerable ideological and religious hiatus between seminary-educated clergy and layfolk, whose theological education and vocabulary may have been gotten on the streets, or more likely on the tube?

Confused and disillusioned, many have either dropped out of the church long ago or still attend only because they appreciate the social atmosphere and friendships developed over the years. They may have given up on religion, but cannot seem to break the habit of going to church. Or it may be a nice place for the children. Or the church has so many activities to choose from—"food, fun and fellowship for those of every age and interest." But as a place which helps them articulate a dynamic faith, it is almost useless.

Many clergy are trapped. Having neglected the theological task for so long, they now feel they don't dare present anything of substance. Why, they might be accused of being "liberals," or of not taking the Bible literally. In clergy meetings, where we have talked seriously about theology, colleagues have said time after time, "I could never get away with telling my people that sort of thing." But what they consider to be a terrible gray problem may instead be a gracious opportunity. Could it be that we have misread the best layfolk among us? Many of our people hunger for something deeper, richer, and more soul-sustaining. They want to understand God as other than an old man on a cloud, who either bails us out of bad situations when we ask or keeps account of our misdeeds. They want to know what Christ means today; what is the work of the Holy Spirit; how we know what is true; what is the authority of Scripture; what is the final word about life—in short, the basic questions theology has traditionally addressed.

In my congregation, I have for a long time seen my major role as theologian in residence. The laity must run the church, its organization and program. That is not my job. I am the rabbi, the teacher. I teach not only on Sunday but also during the week. I take as many church members, or prospective church members, as possible through a three-year program:

(1) Introduction to the Christian Scriptures
(2) Introduction to the Hebrew Scriptures
(3) Building a Biblical Faith—Christian Theology

Over the years, a major problem has been finding texts suitable for these courses. Originally I used one of the popular prepackaged biblical courses, which are easy to teach but severely limited. I subsequently designed my own curriculum for each unit. Fortunately, when we teach the Bible, we have at the ready the basic text and may not need other supportive materials.

The third year, the theological course, posed a different sort of problem. I searched in vain for an adequate text.

A generation or so ago, Hordern's *A Layman's Guide to Protestant Theology* might have been helpful. But very little has been written in recent decades that is substantial, biblical, and includes a hard look at process thought as well as the insights of liberation, feminist, and ethnic theology. Nor have many scholars written in language helpful to the laity. Not finding a text, I decided to develop one.

This book is the result of that endeavor. It may be useful to pastors looking for an introduction to Christian thought that is honest and scholarly, but not in abstract language. It can be used in organized courses of study or read by laypeople independently. It does not talk down to readers. It deals with the Bible honestly, and opens up theology in a way that people who have been through the lectures from which this text has come have found liberating.

I owe a great debt to the members of the First Christian Church in St. Joseph, Missouri, who for almost two decades have affirmed my role as rabbi, pastor, politician, and community activist. They have not only faithfully attended the various courses of study I offered, but have also encouraged me to prepare this book. I am also deeply indebted to clergy colleagues in Chi Alpha, a theological discussion group, who have listened to pieces of this work over the years, and to ecumenical and denominational colleagues, lay and clergy, who spent early mornings in the summer of 1994 reviewing the materials and offering helpful suggestions. Dr. Stephen Cranford, my "Bishop"; Dr. Michael Kinnamon, Dean of Lexington Theological Seminary; and Creath Thorne, a lay member of the congregation I have served in St. Joseph, have been able critics. Wendy, my wife, is an immensely solid practical theologian who never let me get away with what didn't make sense, and whose knowledge of English grammar saved me from multitudes of glaring literary errors.

If there is a great gulf fixed between what ministers learn in seminary and the much more fundamentalistic theological viewpoints many layfolk hold, the fault lies with those of us called to be teachers. We in the mainline church will never recover our sense of power, passion, and identity until we have congregations peopled by those for whom the theological discipline is lively and vital. This book is written to deal with that need.

1

What Is Theology?

This is a book about theology. It is written for layfolk as well as ministers who are interested in rethinking basic Christian presuppositions. It might have particular appeal to those who have left the church, either physically or intellectually, because the church has either been vague about what it believes, or has become mired in a superstitious fiction with which no inquisitive person can possibly live.

Who Are Today's Theologians?

A generation ago many American Christians could cite the names of the world's outstanding religious thinkers: Barth, Niebuhr, Tillich, and Fosdick to name just four. Now ask the typical layperson to name one respected Christian theologian, and you will most often get a blank stare. They may know about Pat Robertson and either think that what he teaches is really the foundation of Christian thought, or are so turned off by that sort of thing they have given up on the Christian enterprise entirely.

2   *Building a Biblical Faith*

In the popular mind "Christian" means born again, or fundamentalistic, or evangelical, or charismatic. What is on "Christian" television, or what is available in your neighborhood "Christian" bookstore, or what is the theological content of the songs played on "Christian" radio? And isn't the "Christian" position on social issues, such as abortion and homosexuality, naturally punitive? Talking about someone else's sins is indeed at the heart of "Christian" conversation. And, of course, "Christians" believe we ought to have official prayers in public schools. Taking a state-sponsored, albeit sectarian, god out of the classroom is widely seen as the triumph of godlessness.

What is the forum for the rational discussion of these concerns and how they relate to wider theological matters? In former days many local mainline parishes could be counted on to be centers of committed, intelligent, theological reflection. That day is almost gone. While there is still much vital Bible study going on in the shrinking and increasingly ignored mainline institution, little attention is being paid to theology. One reason is the abdication of parish clergy from the theological task. Face it, most parish ministers these days do not see themselves as theologians. "Theologians" live in the rarefied atmosphere of seminaries where the erudite talk to each other in some obscure coded language. If the average parish minister was accused of being a theologian, he/she would deny it with an oath! Fewer parish ministers buy and read theological journals these days. Much more popular are books and articles on how an expanded church parking lot can be used in the cause of evangelism, or how to build a church budget, or ways to plan for retirement. Or consider how many hours each week many parish clergy spend peering at their computer screens, full of data about everything and everybody but without the capacity to induce passion or power.

The Role of Parish Clergy

Parish clergy are managers of small businesses, program directors, pastoral counselors, promoters, marketers, public speakers, entertainers—at least that is how they spend their time and what they believe their layfolk want them to be. But the local minister must primarily be the resident theologian, if there is to be one. Layfolk can organize and run parishes—that is their job. Ordained clergy are called to be rabbis, teachers, explicators of the faith and what it means. If they are not, then who will be? And if no one is, is it any wonder that many members of mainline churches are left untaught?

In every mainline denomination there is a growing rift between theologically educated clergy and the laity they serve. The laity—those who remain—are most often conservative, take the Bible literally, identify the gospel with the American way of life. Most of their religious presuppositions come either from the secular culture—with a Christian facade—or from some media misrepresentation of the gospel.

Every denomination has within it these days a cadre of folk who spend their time railing against the ecclesial establishment for abandoning the faith, by which is meant biblical literalism. Whose fault is it that the mainline church has come to such a dismal place? I suspect it is the seminary-educated clergy, who have abandoned their roles as resident theologians and have allowed the laity to assume that Noah really did get all those critters in that boat a few generations after Eden, because that is what the Scriptures say. Instead of dealing up front with these issues, we tend to stammer and backtrack when asked if Christians don't believe the Bible anymore.

What we see as a problem may, however, be God's way of offering a new possibility. Both nature and the human mind abhor vacuums. The current religious vacuity of many mainline churches may be the opportunity for the clergy to reassert their roles as theologians in residence.

Theology: Thinking About God

As we begin this exploration of theology, let's agree on a definition of the term. *Theology* comes from two Greek words: *theos*, meaning God, and *logos*, meaning the word, or thought, or rational discourse. Zoology is rational discourse about animals. Theology is rational discourse about God. It is the active inquiry of a person or a community of faith. In common parlance, theology is expanded to cover a whole host of religious topics. The criteria are that they relate to an understanding of God and are dealt with rationally. Rationality is not the opposite of faith, it is at its center. To speak about God or other religious subjects in dogmatic terms is to speak about theology. But to engage in asking questions, exploring doubts, and raising objections is also to do theology. Doctrine, as opposed to theology, is a body of teachings, and dogma is what you get when doctrine is officially proclaimed. This book is about thoughtful theological inquiry.

Theology, for our purpose, includes thinking not only about God but about the meaning of Christ and the Holy Spirit. It includes notions about authority, particularly the authority of the Scriptures. It discusses the problems of suffering and sin, and how the cross of Christ saves us. It looks at other religions and deals with how we know what is true. It talks about God's activity in everyday life, in history and the end of history.

Christian theology flows from the gospel, the story of God's gracious love and purpose seen in Jesus the Christ. It is rooted in a biblical tradition and is seen in the lives and history of a faithful community.

Throughout the book the point will be made that all of us, especially in a pluralistic society, approach theology with our own cultural and philosophic presuppositions. We will give particular attention to ways the poor may see the work of God, and how women or ethnic minorities approach these issues. We invite all those curious about themselves, their world, and God to join us in this exploration. Some who read may find answers. Others may find a new set of questions. Some may be disturbed, but many more may be relieved that at least one author is willing to put in written form what they have long held to be true but were ashamed or embarrassed to affirm, particularly within their own religious communities. We invite readers to argue with our points of view, to confront, struggle and search. This book seeks not so much to give answers to questions as to open fresh sets of questions and encourage personal exploration. It is a seeker's guide to Christian thought.

The task of theology begins in thinking about God, and to that task we move in Chapter Two.

2

God—
Power with a Purpose

Theology begins with God. The very word *theology* indicates that "the word about God" or "discourse about God" is the root of all theological inquiry. Everything else in theology is derivative of that discipline. Yet even to define God, let alone describe what God is like, seems enshrouded in Mystery. In one sense God is the center of all Mystery, the unknowable, the one who dwells in a light that no one can approach, that which is beyond being, or as Paul Tillich said, "the ground of Being." Hold on, phrases like that will become clear as we go along.

Confronting the Mystery

To discover who or what God is does not solve a mystery— with a small *m*. The Mystery of God is not to be solved! In our scientific age mysteries can be reduced to problems, and problems can be taken care of with enough money and brain power.

Consider how we solved the mystery of the atom. I once lived across the street from what had been the University of Chicago's handball courts. There now stands on that spot a

7

marvelous bronze sculpture by Henry Moore titled, "Atomic Energy." To some it looks like a skull, or a mushroom cloud. To others it pulses with creative energy. In that unlikely location scientists, with unlimited budgets and the world's greatest brain power, solved that mystery and produced the first self-sustained nuclear reaction.

That is not how we will solve the Mystery—capital *M*— that is God. It will not come about at a meeting of the world's best theologians, operating with an unlimited grant from the wealthiest foundation. God will remain a Mystery. *The* Mystery! Nevertheless, we must bring our best thinking, the clearest evidence, the humblest reason to this issue. We must think and talk about God, and see as far as we can into the dimness. In addition, we are spiritual beings, not just bright animals, and cannot simply think about the Mystery that is God, but must enter into relationship with that Mystery—however imperfectly. After all, are we not all incurably religious?

God in Our Midst

On the other hand, perhaps God is not just remote or removed, but rather very much part of what we already know or are gaining knowledge about. Perhaps God is at the heart of the very processes that govern and order our lives and the life of our universe. We may find clues to God in both nature and history. That is to say, God may be clearly revealed to us in ways we can incorporate into our rational and emotional lives. And perhaps we cannot even separate God from the most intimate parts of our daily experiences.

However God has been defined, men and women have been engaged in this theological endeavor ever since our earliest ancestors quaked before the thunder and lightning, and sought to appease whatever power lay behind the terrors of nature. As time went on, more sophisticated "theologians" tried to make sense of and relate to the Mystery other than by simply quaking before its power. By the time we arrived at the earliest Hebrew writings, God was no longer simply a God of nature, standing

apart out there somewhere, detached and awesome. In Jahweh
God was seen as profoundly involved in human history. God
was not only concerned but was also intimately immersed in
the day-to-day events of Israel, and derivatively, of the rest of
the world.

Perhaps the main difference between the followers of Baal
and the followers of Jahweh was this distinction. Jahweh not
only had a people but had also entered into a covenant relationship with them. One could deal with Jahweh, even argue.

God was still related to nature as its creator, but Jahweh was
much more than a nature god to be appeased if the crops were
to grow. By the time the Genesis stories were assembled, a much
later development, the God of nature and the God of history
were seen by a particular group of Semitic people as one God.
But nature, they believed, was created to serve the purposes of
history. That is, God created the physical universe and humankind, which was part of a unitive whole, in such a way that
there could exist a relationship—a covenant. The natural world
was not incidental, and neither was humankind. "I will be your
God, and you will be my people." This God participated with
them in the most ordinary day-to-day experiences of their lives.
What we may believe to be primitive laws and regulations describe the interrelationship. What to eat and wear, how to con-
struct their buildings for worship, and how to treat a skin rash
were all part of the relationship.

Creative Power with a Purpose

What's more, these Hebrew foreparents of ours believed that
the creation was not just willy-nilly. It was orderly, and even
beyond that, it was benevolent. In one mythic story, recorded
in Genesis, it was said that at the end of the first creative day
God looked at what had been made and said, "It is good." At
the end of the sixth day God said, "It is very good." Into this
early theological model we therefore see incorporated two attributes: creative power, or energy; and a benevolent purpose,
or goodness. Perhaps these ancient people came up with the

best definition of God anyone has had before or since. At least they had the basic building blocks identified. *God: power with a benevolent purpose.*

This energy was not just chaotic; it was headed somewhere. It had a direction, and that direction was pro-humankind and pro-creation. History was in motion positively, and whatever the course of the creative energy, God not only dictated the process but could be identified with the process.

Not only that, God created a universe—one whole entire thing. Or could we say with these foreparents of ours, that we have at the heart of our faith One Good Power? Thus:

(1) Not many gods, but one God.
(2) Not a divided creation, but a universe.
(3) Not a chaotic creation, but an orderly one.
(4) Not an ethically neutral or disinterested God, but one good God. God is a force, always moving ahead and upward, always operating with some end in view.
(5) Not a cosmic struggle between good and evil, light and darkness, but one creative God, whose authority extends over evil and darkness.

The God Who Looks Like Us

The difficulty with that definition, however, lies in our inability to develop a personal relationship with energy, even benevolent energy. We can relate to a person. It is very hard to address a power plant. Over the ensuing centuries, therefore, religious people tended to define God more in human terms. Seeing God with attributes similar to our own makes God accessible. God, in the common mind, became much like a very powerful human being. To our foreparents there seemed to be few ways to describe God other than to talk about the hand of God, the heart of God, the will of God. God is just like us, only much more so. While these personal notions about God have been helpful, we must realize that they are our creations.

This big person God had to be located someplace. The Hebrew people always believed that God lived just above the highest mountains—since the covering over the earth, called the firmament, was somewhere up there. At least that is where "He" could be found. People communicated with God by going to the mountains.

"I lift my eyes to the hills—from where will my help come? My help comes from the LORD, who made heaven and earth" (Psalm 121:1–2). Moses went to the mountain to get The Ten Commandments. Jerusalem's temple was built on Mount Zion. Jesus talked to Moses and Elijah from one mountain, and ascended to heaven from another. Even the giving of his most famous short collection of teachings, according to Matthew, was on a mountain. Heaven, where God lived, therefore, must be just higher than the tallest hill. The Greeks had always known that the gods cavorted on Mt. Olympus.

While it is helpful to talk about God in terms of person and place, these metaphors severely limited what many early theologians thought about God. God became so much like them that the Mystery dissolved with the familiarity. Thus, despite the best efforts by later theologians, who refused to limit God to human terms and a physical place, I daresay most Christians even today are stuck with this very limited and mundane idea of God.

Over the years I have asked laypersons, and ministers as well, to define or describe God. One gets a series of images which tend to trap God in ways we might describe important human beings. God is powerful. God is creator. God is provider. God sustains the world. God is loving, an attribute best seen in Jesus. God is sovereign, is judge, is the final arbiter of history.

While these images hint at the truth, they all tend to reduce God to a character just a little bigger than human size. To compound the matter, we also have become used to other linguistic images of God that reinforce that notion. God, for instance, is male, "He." Since we cannot think of any human being without assigning gender, and since most of the literature was produced by males, and since language is not an exact science, God has become very much a He. God also takes on the coloration of the political system of the day. So we get this male God as a King or a Lord. Both of these metaphors were easily understood by those living in political kingdoms or feudal states. It is just another illustration of how we tend to describe things, even God, in terms we know best.

If we realize that the Mystery is essentially a Mystery, and we will never fully understand it or unscrew the inscrutable, none of these images, though useful, can be taken with final seriousness. In fact, no images of God, not even our best ones, can be taken with final seriousness. All theology, which must communicate by using commonly understood symbols (language being the primary example), only points to a reality beyond itself.

The problem is, we tend to take our symbols seriously, and are subsequently stuck with them. We assume they are orthodox, the substance of the faith, the understanding of God posited by an infallible and inerrant Bible, the way God must be, and forget they are only figures of speech, thoroughly conditioned by the cultures that produced them.

This is not a new problem. In 1964 J. B. Phillips, a Bible scholar and theologian of some note, published a best-selling book called *Your God Is Too Small*. In this thin book Phillips first described all the limited and limiting images of God he believed most people held. Phillips was too kind to say that folks still assumed that God was an old man with a great white beard, who sat on a cloud with a book on his lap in which he inscribed the good and evil deeds of earth folk.

The embarrassing fact, however, is that this is exactly what substantial numbers of Christians thought then and still do. God is either that or an oblong blur without content or shape. While Phillips alludes briefly to this "Grand Old Man" notion, it is only one of thirteen equally immature and inadequate views of God. There are the Managing Director, the Resident Police-man, and the Pale Galilean, among others.

The second half of Phillips' book was an attempt to refocus Christian thought about God in ways that escape the too small God he earlier described. While Phillips hints at a more mature understanding of God, many who read the book understood what he was lamenting in the first half, but had a difficult time coming to terms with what he was describing in the final sections.

How Do You Pray to a Process?

If we are to understand God as power with a purpose, the verb—the *doing*, not just the *doer*—the energy of creation that is forever lifting, moving and saving—that is making whole, how do we enter into a personal relationship with "Him," or "it"? It is one thing to pray to a loving father in heaven. It is cold and impersonal to be held in the grasp of a life force, or what the philosopher Henri Bergson called the "Elan Vital." By that Bergson meant that vital urge at the heart of everything, which makes us grow and transforms this wandering planet into a the-ater of unending creativity. Yet pray we must, for there can be no religion of worth that relates us only to a mindless and soul-less machine. We will deal with this issue more thoroughly in the chapters on Jesus the Christ and the Holy Spirit. But we cannot avoid mentioning it here.

How, for instance, do we utter any prayer, and to whom or what, and with what expected result? Is it only a matter of talk-ing to ourselves? Does anything really happen when we pray? If by prayer we mean changing the mind and intention of God, the problem persists. If we are at point "A" and God is at point "B" and we mean by prayer getting God's attention so that we lure "Him" over to where we are (1), so that the power might flow (2), we are reduced to a definition of God that is neither helpful nor accurate.

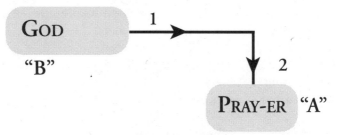

If, however, we are at point "A" and God is at point "B," and prayer is our effort to identify with the source of the power flow (2)—this power with a purpose—and it is we who are moved (1), then our definition of God rests on more solid ground.

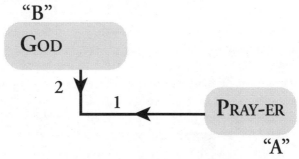

There have been times when I could see a good wind rippling the waters offshore as I tried to move my sailboat, the *John Mark*, across Maine's Penobscot Bay. Trying to lure the wind to the cove where I sat almost becalmed didn't accomplish much. I could call—or pray—to the wind until I was voiceless, without results. When with what breeze was available I got the *John Mark* to where the winds were blowing fresh and strong, everything changed and I was lifted to where both my craft and the winds were headed. The problem was not to get the wind to me, but to get me to the wind.

And yet, quite apart from anything I could do, there were those occasions when I could see the ripples coming closer and closer, and I was engulfed in a sustaining breeze I neither conjured nor had earned.

Prayer changes things. Liberals have been fond of saying that prayer changes the one who prays. While that is correct, it is not the whole story. If I find the source of power, and plug my life into that source, not only do I change, but the possibility arises for much around me to change. The lights can come on, for one thing! Getting our lives in harmony with the divine purpose will not only make me feel better, it can heal, make whole, and redeem. Prayer is more than an internal rational exercise in talking to ourselves, hoping that we get some clarity. It may be that, but it is much more. Prayer brings us into harmony with the source of all goodness—the One Good God, "maker of heaven and earth."

Prayer also opens all the possibilities God is continually offering. God continues to create and moves with us from one moment to another. The miracle is that when we are attuned to God's purpose we live on the cusp of the possible. We are not stuck with the obvious. With God we live on the edge of what is not yet. A new world of potential occasions is perpetually open to us.

In the various religions of the world, including the Christian religion, mystics have always known they could enter the will and the mind of God as they hold in check their own wills. Mystics sense they do not have to understand God to become part of the mind of God, just lose their own egos in a quest to abide in the unknowable. The first impulse to be abandoned is the belief that one can change God's mind. God has already acted on our behalf. The response is ours. It is in the dynamic interaction between what God has done and our response that the miracle happens and new life emerges.

Jesus, in the garden of Gethsemane, sought the will of God—sought to submerge his will in that of the one he called "Father." Jesus did not seek to alter God's plan. At least, having made that petition, "Let this cup pass from me," he was able to say, "Not my will but thine be done." The essence of prayer may be seeking the divine will—tapping into the power source. And that can change your life and the world around you.

Ultimately we must encounter a God with whom we and the community of faith live in covenant. Thus we know and are related to God through Jesus the Christ—all of God we can see and know in human form, and the Holy Spirit—God at work in our world and in our lives. More about these two concerns later.

However we begin to think about God, we must do it starting from where we are, as must everyone who does theology in every age and every culture. And we are limited—in time, space, history, culture, philosophy, scientific understanding, genetic makeup and social structure. Scholars can transcend these limitations, somewhat, but theology—thinking about God—cannot be limited to scholars. The purpose of this book is to provide some tools by which every thoughtful Christian can be a theologian. We are assisted in this exploration by a biblical witness, a tradition, and a community of faith. Ours is not a solitary exploration, or one limited to our time and place.

When we think about God, therefore, we must do so realizing we are caught in our limitations. All our thinking and symbolizing will be proximate—not ultimate. That is, we will never find or be able to articulate the whole truth, only the truth as we see it from within the limitations imposed by who we are. That should not overly trouble us. We have already concluded that no matter how profound we are, or claim to be, there is that about God that is always far beyond us, and our words and ideas are only shadows of the infinite. This does not stop us in our quest to understand that which is Mystery. It simply saves us from spiritual, intellectual, and religious arrogance. The faithful response must always lie in the testimony of the community, not in the wisdom of the self.

Does God Have Other Sheep?

Once we make that admission, we humbly realize that other people in other times and cultures, operating under other philosophic structures and cultural understandings, may authentically think about God in ways very different from the ways we do. That is not to reduce theology to some inane lowest common denominator such as, "All paths lead up the same mountain," or, "It doesn't matter what you believe as long as you are sincere." Theology is a discipline that excludes sloppy thought. It does, however, cause us to recognize that when those of other cultures understand or relate to God in ways we find outside our experience, it is not our task to make them see it our way, or consider them in error.

I am often asked, "Are there other ways to come to God than by Jesus?" I reply, "Not for me!" My life has been shaped by a tradition that flows from the record of God's gracious action in Jesus the Christ. I do not start with a philosophy or a point of view, but with a gospel—an act of God. Nevertheless, I have shed the arrogance that says that God is limited to a first-century Jew who never got a hundred miles or thirty-four years from his birthplace and time. I am bound, therefore, to listen humbly to the experience of others and to celebrate with them that as I have experienced the Mystery I call God, so may have they.

The task of theology must always be done humbly. The arrogant alternative is to assume we have been given all wisdom, can know the unknowable, and have reduced the Mystery to a set of intellectual problems to be figured out by those as wise as we are. The thesis of this book is that the theological task is posited on just the opposite assumption.

3

Jesus the Christ—
All of God We Can See

The two most difficult issues in Christian theology are: (1) If God is all-good and all-powerful, why is there evil in the world? (2) Who was Jesus and what was his relationship to God? We will examine the first question in Chapter Seven. This chapter will focus our attention on Jesus.

"Fully Human—Fully God":
How the Church "Fathers" Saw It

For many centuries the early church struggled to define who Jesus was and whether, or to what extent, or in what way he was God. The issue was complicated by a number of factors. Even the four Gospel writers saw Jesus in ways that differed dramatically from each other. For theologians who lived in the first centuries after Jesus, theology was necessarily seen in terms of a Greek philosophic system, or notions about the world and what is real. Theology and philosophy are always inseparable. People inevitably draw notions of God from a particular worldview. While all Christian theology begins with the gospel, to which testimony is given in the scriptural record, it passes through and is colored by particular philosophic traditions.

19

If one's notion of the cosmos places the earth in the center, the waters below and the heavens or firmament above, and if up is good and if God is good, then it follows that God is up. In Chapter Two we began to see some of the implications drawn from this view of the world, as ancient people sought to discover who or what God was.

More important than the particular direction in which God could be located, was the conviction that God must live *somewhere,* just like every person must live or be somewhere. And if God is somewhere, then God exists in much the same way we exist. God is another being. Or substitute the word *person* for *being.* God is a person.

It is obvious that Jesus is also a person, who walked on this earth and bore all the marks of personhood—physical and spiritual. If Jesus is a person, and God is a person—and if Jesus is at the same time God—then God is at least two persons. Don't panic at the complexity of that sentence, just read it again and follow it from one proposition to another. Add the Holy Spirit, who is also God, and you get three persons. Presto! You have growing out of this philosophic structure, one God and three persons—or the Trinity.

But the church fathers, the name we give to theologians of the first several Christian centuries, insisted there was only one God—one entity that was substantially God. There are not three Gods, only three persons interwoven in one substance. Careful—there are not three substances—just one. But all three persons are the same God, otherwise the door might be left open for three Gods. Jesus' substance and God's substance are not just *similar* to each other. They are the *same.* The argument about this matter of substance and persons went on for a long time, until the majority of those in a series of Councils of the whole church settled the matter, if not for all times, at least to their satisfaction.

Mind you, all the time the majority of these leaders asserted that Jesus was fully human—just like us. Nevertheless, his humanity did not compromise his substantial identity—that is, his absolute oneness—with God.

Along the way other ideas theologians put forward were discarded for a variety of good reasons we don't need to go into at any length. The first heresy was that if Jesus were really God, not just like God, then he could not have been a human being, could not have been born, could not have suffered and died. All of the events identifying him as a physical being were illusions. They didn't really happen. They just seemed to happen. God, they held, was a spiritual being, and since all things fleshly were evil, probably created by an evil lesser deity or a fallen angel, Jesus could not have really been human. He just appeared to be flesh and blood.

"No!" said the church of the first century. Jesus was fully human. The little letter in Christian Scriptures we call 2 John puts it this way: "Many deceivers have gone out into the world, those who do not confess that Jesus Christ has come in the flesh; any such person is the deceiver and the antichrist!" (2 John 7).

Early in the second century, when the first extended statement we can identify as a creed was written, the point was clearly made, He was *born* of the Virgin Mary, *suffered* under Pontius Pilate, was *crucified, dead, and buried.* Note the verbs. It was not the virgin birth that was being affirmed as much as it was the fact of birth. He was more than an appearance, a seemingness, smoke and mirrors. Jesus was born, suffered, and died. Therefore, he was fully human. Unlike in more modern times, most folks back then had little trouble believing in his divinity. Their problem was believing in his humanity.

Later a number of theologians theorized that he *became* God, even though he was born as a human. One group held he was a good man—so good that God adopted him, made him God or at least God's son—although the latter term was not carefully defined. Again the church said, "No!" He was God for all times and even before all times. He neither achieved that status by his goodness, nor did God adopt him. None of this, however, denied his full humanity.

Others tried to solve the problem by dividing Jesus in half. Half of him was God and half of him was human. But the question as to which half did what satisfied nobody, and in the long run the church affirmed that he was "fully man and fully God," without division.

Nor did the orthodox buy the notion that Jesus was God in a human body, or that he was something like God. He was fully God and fully human, and any other way to describe him was heresy.

The problem is that these ideological constructs make sense only if you understand the world like the classical Greek thinkers and their philosophic descendants understood it. If, however, the way one thinks about the world doesn't include the difficult notions of substance and persons, then few of the questions the theologians fretted over for centuries are critical for us and for our day. We have a very different way to understand reality.

Jesus, and How We See the World

In our era we are not bound by the sort of philosophic or scientific world that conditioned how the church fathers thought. The sun no longer rotates around the earth, and heaven is no longer up. What is more, we don't draw the same distinction they did between substance and persons. Something is really whatever it is, and not what the perfect heavenly form or idea of it is.

If you go back and read Chapter Two, about God, and understand God in terms of energy—power with a purpose, a process, and not a being as we are beings—then few of the problems concerning the relationship between Jesus and God will consume your attention. To allow them to determine how you understand Jesus would be like a physicist who frets about how the universe is constructed, without taking into account quantum mechanics. The world was not seen in the same way by those who had nothing more than Newton's laws to go by. Any modern attempt to understand the universe using Newtonian mechanics would be just as futile as trying to understand Jesus/God/Holy Spirit using the philosophic system—way of thinking—that was operative in the fifth century. But remember as you consider your worldview, these early theologians did not start with a philosophic system. They started with the biblical witness. The doctrine of the Trinity was an attempt to make sense out of the Scriptures using a contemporary worldview as the vehicle.

It should not be assumed that the creeds of the church, and these great arguments in our theological history, are useless. We are the products of what we have been. We are children of history, and these discussions still tell the truth, but only in terms of the philosophy through which the fathers looked. If you are not terribly concerned or dominated by Plato's world of forms, or the difference between substance and person—or object—you probably don't lie awake at night wondering about the mystery of the Trinity or the exact meaning of the Athanasian Creed. Nevertheless, these formulations are still used and useful as they trace the development of faith from the New Testament to ways in which we think about Jesus in our era.

The foregoing discussion is also important because much of the Christian world, from Catholicism to Orthodoxy, as well as a considerable portion of Protestant mainline religion, still proceeds on the basis of the great creeds whose major findings we have sketched above. There have been, however, three other ways to think about who Jesus is and what may be his relationship to God. We will now briefly sketch them.

The Jesus of History

From time to time in church history, scholars and theologians have been fascinated with putting together a solid biography of Jesus. The task of creating an accurate account of the life of this first-century Galilean is not as easy as it might appear. The assumption that one can sit down with the Gospels—Matthew, Mark, Luke, and John—and develop a coherent life story grows more difficult with every discovery made about how these documents developed. Not only do the four Gospels disagree with one another, but we are now fairly clear that each grew out of perspectives diverse parts of the church wanted to identify and problems each needed to address. Yet the early church never appeared troubled by these differences.

Luke, the Gentile advocate of God's universal compassion, and Matthew, the spiritually oriented Messianic Jew, do not just differ in detail, they differ in basic facts regarding Jesus' life. Consider, for example, how each handles the Beatitudes. With Matthew it is, "Blessed are those who hunger and thirst for righteousness…" (Matthew 5:6). Luke takes the same collection of sayings and hears Jesus saying, "Blessed are you who are hungry now…" (Luke 6:21). It is more than a simple difference in words. The fact that Matthew puts the sermon on a mountain and Luke places the event down on a level place says more about the perspectives of those who collected and edited these sayings than a modest alteration in geography. As we have seen, for Jews God was identified with mountains, and everything important took place on them: Mt. Sinai, Mt. Zion, Mt. Nebo, the Mount of Olives, the Mount of Transfiguration, the Mount of the Ascension. But Christians in the Greek world, such as Luke, wanted to get away from the notion that God—like the exotic deities of Olympus—cavorted on mountains. Besides, on the plain everybody stood on equal ground. Matthew seems concerned with spiritual hunger, Luke with physical hunger! And what is more, for Luke God's Reign was for the poor, not just for those on a spiritual quest.

This example is a drop in the ocean of difficulties involved in any attempt to recreate a historically accurate biography of Jesus. What you have are four dissimilar cultural points of view, each with its own needs and each taking the stories of and about Jesus and fitting them into specific cultural presuppositions.

Perhaps for some readers the question is now raised, "Well, if you can't take the Gospels literally or as authentic history, what is the authority of the Scriptures?" We will get to the critical issue in Chapter Five.

Nevertheless, the quest to discover the Jesus of history persists. For many of us today it seems far simpler and productive to let the Gospels speak about Jesus than to wade through the labyrinth described earlier in this chapter.

Almost a hundred years ago Albert Schweitzer produced a massive book entitled *A Quest for the Historical Jesus*. After an exhaustive effort, Schweitzer concluded that it was impossible to pierce the mist and that, "he comes to us as one unknown."

In the mid-1990s a group of scholars attempted to determine which of the words ascribed to Jesus may be authentic and which are not. While their approach was radically skeptical and they concluded that practically nothing in our red-lettered editions of the New Testament can be clearly ascribed to the lips of Jesus, nevertheless this panel demonstrated how difficult it is to etch out a clear picture of the man of Galilee.

With all their difficulties, however, the Gospels may provide more clues to the one we call Jesus the Christ than attempts to reenter the philosophic world that led to the Trinity and the creeds. We may get different pictures of him in the Four Gospels, but each of them adds immeasurably to our sense of who he was and what he means today. To be fixated on the differences may not be fruitful. What is productive is to see how the early church, which developed these documents within a few decades of his life, understood him.

The Messiah

A second alternative to dealing with the creeds and their production as the way to understand Jesus, is to examine the meaning of the title, "Christ." While we all realize that Christ is not Jesus' last name—like the "Jones," in John Jones—we have not been as clear in defining what that designation or title means. Efforts to see Jesus as God by assuming that "Christ" equals "God," are doomed to failure.

Christ is simply the Greek translation of the Hebrew word *Messiah*. To say that Jesus is the Christ is to affirm that he is the fulfillment of Jewish expectations. Nowhere back then did anyone believe that the Messiah was God. In fact, for Jews, radical monotheists, who hesitated to verbalize the name *God* or even write it out, it would have been the height of blasphemy to affirm that Messiah was God. By the time the church got around to defining who Jesus was, in terms of a Greek philosophic structure, the Jewish roots of the faith had become so detached it did not seem to occur to these theologians that to equate Christ and God was a major contradiction.

The word *Messiah* means "the anointed one." While variations on the Messianic theme were as numerous for Jews as the meaning of Jesus was for Christians, the notion that the Messiah and God were the same was not one of them. The Messiah was most often imaged as a kingly person who would reoccupy David's throne and reestablish an earthly authority. While not always viewed as a political leader, it is impossible to separate the notion of Messiah from the aspirations of Israel, a political entity. The image that Messiah was to be a suffering servant struck only a minor cord in the history of Messianism.

The Gospels make it clear that Jesus redefined the notion of Messiah, and the early church's use of the title "Christ" took messiahship out of the political arena—"My kingdom is not from this world" (John 18:36). While the Christian faith cannot be reduced to Jewish Messianism, to see Jesus as the Messiah and not take into account hundreds of years of messianic tradition is to deal dishonestly with our Jewish roots.

Jesus came proclaiming the kingdom or reign of God, which was very different from the kingdom most of his contemporaries thought the Messiah would inaugurate. It is, however, a difficult leap to see Jesus not only as the one anointed by God to proclaim the advent of the new age, but also as God in the flesh. Not even the church, which produced the synoptic Gospels, came to that very unJewish conclusion. By the time the Fourth Gospel was assembled, we have the church already struggling with the philosophic questions described at the beginning of this chapter, having abandoned most, if not all, of its Jewish linkage. With that departure from its roots also went much of the early church's concern with the Jesus of history.

The image of the Christ or the Messiah is helpful for us if

we understand that Jesus so embodied the mind, spirit and energy of God that he could declare that God's purpose was to bring a new public reality into being.

All of God We Can See

We now turn to a third alternate way to understand Jesus and his relationship to God. This approach also requires that we put aside the presuppositions about the nature of reality—substance and person—which conditioned how the church fathers dealt with the problem. It flows from an understanding of God similar to the way we put it in Chapter Two. God is not a being who lives somewhere, nor an entity totally separated from the dynamics of the world. God is not understood in philosophic terms such as "all-knowing," "all-powerful" and "all-present." God is power with a purpose. God is the energy that drives everything; always refining, moving toward a goal. We call that goal the reign or kingdom of God, and we call the process that drives it, love. God is love—the *action*, not the *principle*. While love may be a very human-centered way to describe the nature of God, we have no better word. It is also a word with which the Scriptures are intimately familiar. Love is the creative, dynamic force that is continually at work reconciling all things and restoring what has been broken.

We affirm that Jesus both understood and embodied that love. He was love in the flesh. If God is essentially love in action and Jesus is love embodied, then if we cannot call Jesus "God" in the way the church fathers did, we can understand that: *Jesus is all of God we can see in human form. In Jesus we discover all of God we can know. In Jesus we have all of God we need.* If you want to understand how God operates in the world, what it means that this power with a purpose functions in history, look at Jesus as pictured in the Gospels and in the history of the church. While our way of doing theology hesitates to cite specific texts to prove points, the notion that in Jesus we see all of God we can understand is remarkably compatible with many Christological passages of the New Testament.

"For in him all the fullness of God was pleased to dwell" (Colossians 1:19). "In Christ God was reconciling the world to himself" (2 Corinthians 5:19a). "Whoever has seen me has seen the Father" (John 14:9b). "I am the way, and the truth, and the life" (John 14:6a).

While the word is symbolic, we can understand what Jesus meant when he called God *Father.* The rhetorical quagmire one must wade through to understand how Jesus could pray to God if they were the same substance—and most of the rest of the problems the church fathers encountered—are dramatically overcome. Jesus' full humanity is maintained, but so also is the full expression of what God is—if God is the verb we call energy/love—power with a purpose. We also avoid the sense that God is a being out there somewhere beyond the sunset. God is closer than breathing and nearer than hands or feet. Indeed, our breath, the power that enlivens us, the love that is the end product of history, the Omega point toward which history and our lives move, is God. And all of that we understand through Jesus.

Jesus can be Sovereign and Savior without the weight of having to filter everything through fifth-century Greek thought. We can participate in the energy of the universe as we participate in the love that created and sustains it.

Furthermore, religion is not just knowing about Jesus, for that is little more than an intellectual pursuit. The Christian faith must move beyond mere rationality. The Christian religion is the embodiment of that love—becoming as much as we can like Jesus. No one can be an authority on love by reading books about it. I can write a hundred doctoral dissertations on the meaning of love, but I won't know the first thing about love until I am loved by a person I love in return. Not only do all the commandments hang on the love of God and the love of neighbor, as Jesus said, but so does all theology. The difference is that theology begins with the affirmation, "In this is love, not that we loved God, but that [God] loved us" (1 John 4:10a).

How do we know that the world created and sustained by this energy we call God is a safe, caring place? You won't easily find it by looking at nature. Nature tends to operate by the law of tooth and fang. It is not particularly friendly. Ask the victims of earthquakes and floods about that. We know the world is a safe, loving place by looking at Jesus. The golden text of the Bible doesn't say that [God] loved the world so much we were given the laws of nature, or atomic energy, or the principles of physics. It says, God loved the world so much a Son was given (John 3:16a).

If God is power with a purpose, the dynamic impulse in creation, and the loving energy that moves the world along its path to fulfillment, we are tied to that purpose and plan by Jesus—his life, his teachings, his trust in God. If I am to know, finally, anything about God, somebody has to show me by living that life. I've got to see it in the flesh. That's what Jesus does. I won't find it in a book. I won't discover it in an institution. I won't absorb it in obedience to law. Book, church, and commandment help point the way. Finally, I can know it only in action—in a life lived—in a person.

For Christians, Jesus is that person. He is all of God we can understand in human form. In Jesus we discover all of God we can know. In Jesus we have all of God we need. God's plan and purpose is fleshed out in him.

Do other people in other cultures and religions find God in other ways? I don't believe God's love and power are limited to Christians. But that is the wrong question. What we do know is that for us—in terms we can understand—God has been revealed in Jesus, and that is all we need.

Who Is Christ for Us Today?

We now have described four ways we can understand who Jesus was:

(1) seeing his relationship to God through the church fathers and the ecumenical creeds;

(2) attempting to reconstruct a biography of the historic Jesus;

    (3) examining the Jewish roots and the nature of his messiahship—his Christhood;

    (4) finding in him the purposeful power of love lived out—the power we call God.

All of these avenues are open to us. The real questions, however, are not the academic queries as to his relationship to God, or how we develop an authentic biography, or how to understand the nature of Jewish Messiahship, or even how we define him in terms of God's love. The ultimate Christological question was put by Dietrich Bonhoeffer from his prison cell: "Who is Christ for us today?" That question will be answered differently by every individual and by every culture. We will never capture God, or Jesus, in our theological categories or rational boxes.

In his book *Jesus Through the Centuries*, Jaroslav Pelikan reviews the various ways in which people across the ages have understood Jesus. Some of the images Pelikan cites are: Rabbi, King of Kings, Christ Crucified, Monk, Universal Man, Mirror of the Eternal, Prince of Peace, Teacher of Common Sense, Liberator. Each image contains its own richness, and helps us understand the fullness of God—as God was in Jesus. How one enlarges a particular image in one circumstance and diminishes it in another will flow from the historical and philosophic viewpoint of that person or culture. Finally each person and culture must ask, "What does Jesus mean for me and my times? Who is Christ for us today?" To deal with that question, and follow where it leads, is the reason any believer does theology.

4

The Holy Spirit—
God in Our Midst

The orthodox—Catholic, Protestant, and Eastern—use the designation "Holy Spirit" widely. Protestant and Catholic charismatics not only use the word, but feel deeply moved and enriched by the "gifts of the Spirit," "the baptism of the Spirit," and "the indwelling power of the Spirit." Many mainline Protestants, while they still use the word, seem to have little grasp of what the Spirit is or does.

One needs only to reread the early paragraphs about Jesus in Chapter Three to discover the roots of our confusion. If the Holy Spirit is God—indeed one of the three persons that make up the one God—and there is no difference in substance—(remember how the church fathers viewed substance) between God and the Holy Spirit, yet the Holy Spirit is a separate unique entity...well, you how see the quagmire gets deeper and deeper. The only less difficult matter is that, unlike Jesus, there is nothing human, or physical, about the Holy Spirit. It is pure Spirit, without flesh and without a particular—and therefore limited—location in history. And yet in the trinitarian formula, the Holy Spirit does not perform a unique function. The church has always held that the Spirit is creator, redeemer, and sustainer, just as are the Father and Son.

As with Jesus, there is no way to untangle this knot as long as we insist on using an ancient philosophic system as the foundation for the discussion. It will be easier for us if we put aside the perspective the church fathers employed and go at the problem without the encumbrance of viewing the matter based on a worldview with which we are no longer conversant.

The Spirit as God's Activity and Presence

Let us think of the Holy Spirit in this way: *the Holy Spirit is the name we give to the activity of God in our world and in our midst.* Or: *the Holy Spirit is the power and presence of God in history and in our lives.* When we talk about the Spirit of God, and the purposeful creative energy of God, we are talking about the same thing.

Sometimes I call her "Wendy" and sometimes I call her "my wife," or "mother" (with the children), or "teacher" (with her students), but I am always naming the same person. When we want to describe God as active in our lives or present in our world, we may simply use the word *God,* or we may refer to the *Holy Spirit* or the *Spirit of God.*

No Christian I know questions that God—in old language, the first person of the Trinity—was the creator of the world. The Apostles Creed affirms in its initial sentence, "I believe in God the Father Almighty, Creator of heaven and earth." But the very first verses of Genesis speak of the *Spirit* of God moving over the void and accomplishing the creation (Genesis1:2b). One can just as easily say that it was the Holy Spirit that did the creating. Remember that the Old Testament does not refer to God as Father. That language comes to us through Jesus. For us to speak of God the Father as creator and the Holy Spirit as creator is to say the same thing. Insofar as creation is concerned, the words are interchangeable.

And who created Adam and Eve, the first mythical human beings—or who created the first real human beings, for that matter? It was God. But in Genesis 2:7 we read that these creatures became human when the Spirit of God was breathed into them. Throughout the Scriptures the Holy Spirit, or the Spirit of God, is seen as the power that makes things happen—that which animates, gives life. Thus many Christians have believed that God sent the Holy Spirit and that the Spirit was therefore the agent of God—the way God did what was done. So the Spirit became God doing, or God the doer.

One of the most difficult doctrinal problems the church had was the centuries-long debate about whether the Holy Spirit proceeded (that is, was sent) from the Father, as the Eastern church thought, or from the Father *and* the Son, as the Western church thought. The issue had partly to do with how theologians understood the way the Trinity was constructed, and partly with the right of the Western church to change the creed! That is, it was as much a political as a theological debate. While there were other issues separating Rome and Constantinople, this difficulty provided ammunition on both sides for the final explosive division between Catholic and Orthodox expressions of the faith.

When I was in a Greek monastic community at Mt. Athos a few years back, the monks wanted to know which of these alternate doctrines I believed. It took me a few moments to remember which side in the great schism held to which position. I then made the glaring mistake of suggesting that it really didn't matter. Well, it mattered to theologians fourteen centuries ago, and it matters to the Orthodox church today. Nevertheless, those of us in the West probably lose very little sleep fretting about how and from whom the Holy Spirit proceeds.

It may be much more productive to think of the Holy Spirit as a way to talk about God's activity. While the church fathers, working with their "substance and person" philosophic framework, insisted that God and the Spirit were two different persons while being essentially united, we do not need to engage in those mental exercises. For all practical purposes, when we talk about God, or the Spirit of God, we are talking about the same reality.

When we modern Christians think about God the Father, it is the creative power and process we have in mind—-power with a purpose. When we think of how this power operates in our lives and in our midst, we will tend to use the term *Holy Spirit*. But there is no substantial difference. Which term we use depends on the context. But it is best to keep in mind that we are not talking about two distinct realities. Perhaps that, at heart, is what the church fathers really meant when they said that there were three persons but only one substance.

If there is any distinction in the way the words seem to be used in the New Testament, when Jesus is talking about the relationship of God either to nature or to himself, he uses the word *God* or *Father*. When he is talking about how God will be with the apostles when he, Jesus, is gone, he tends to use the term *The Holy Spirit*. When the New Testament church talks otherwise about the Holy Spirit, it usually refers to God's activity in the world and in the lives of the faithful. The Holy Spirit is most often at work doing something to or with somebody—like filling them, giving them power, sending them on a mission. But then other references just say "God" or "the Father." The Spirit God sends is God's presence.

The word *Spirit*, in both the Hebrew of the Old Testament and the Greek of the New Testament, means *breath*, or *wind*. The breath of God stirred the waters at creation (Genesis 1:2b). God breathed into the first humans and they became living souls (Genesis 2:7). Jesus said that the Spirit blows where it will. No one sees it, knows when it will come or where it goes, but everyone can observe the effects (John 3:8). The Spirit descended on the apostles on the day of Pentecost and was perceived as the rushing of a mighty wind (Acts 2:2).

The Spirit is not predictable. It is impossible to nail it down. It doesn't exist specifically in any place—like heaven or the temple. God is not best worshiped either in Samaria or in Jerusalem because "God is spirit, and those who worship him must worship in spirit and truth" (John 4:24).

When we think of God, this power with a purpose, we tend

to image it acting quite apart from us. The systems that make the world turn are not dependent on any human activity. Yet they are intimately involved with us, part of us as we are part of them. While some theologians have historically seen God as "wholly other," other theologians have held that God has no reality apart from the relationship between God and humanity, and with the created world.

When God acts specifically, or pro-acts in the lives of persons, the term often used in the New Testament is *Holy Spirit*. It blows where it will, not where we decide it should. We do not conjure it and we do not control it. The Spirit comes upon us and we are filled, not by our whim or initiative, but by God's. Theologians could then talk about God's grace as operating independently of any human desire. Thus, God working through the Spirit is sovereign.

If the Spirit is always with us, there are specific times when we are more aware of this presence of God. From early in the history of worship, a sentence asking for the presence of the Holy Spirit has been employed during the prayer of consecration of the bread and wine.

Being Filled with the Spirit

That of God which we call the Holy Spirit is powerfully recognized in a community open to its presence. Haven't there been times when you have been filled to overflowing with a sense of the holy? Or do you remember being empowered to give a gift, make a sacrifice, take a stand, say the right word? Perhaps you have prayed for courage and been filled with courage. Well, that is what the New Testament refers to as being filled with the Spirit. Here in our midst and in our lives comes God's powerful, purposeful presence. The Greek word, which we translate "baptized," simply means to be overwhelmed, submerged, engulfed. To be baptized by or in the Holy Spirit is to be completely taken over or immersed in God's presence. And yet the church has consistently maintained that the Holy Spirit comes to "us," not just to "me."

Charismatic Christians may have overplayed and miscon-
strued the baptism of the Holy Spirit, but mainline Christians
have underplayed and ignored it. The significant text, Acts 2,
describes an event that took place fifty days after Passover and
Jesus' death, during the Feast of Pentecost, or first fruits. Pentecost was one of the three annual occasions for which Jews from
all over the world—meaning basically the shores of the Mediterranean—would make a pilgrimage to Jerusalem. If they did
not come for every feast, they tried to make it at least once a
year. Pentecost drew a large and variegated assembly.

After ten days of prayerful preparation, the apostles waded
into the crowds of pilgrims and preached about Jesus. Only
Peter's sermon is recorded, but all the apostles shared in the
proclamation. The text says that no matter where they were
from, the assembled Jews heard the apostles speaking in their
own language.

Whatever the nature of the sermons, they were not given in
the "heavenly" utterances charismatic Christians refer to as
"speaking in tongues." When these tongues are used today either in public worship or personal devotions, rarely does anyone even claim to understand what is said. On the day of Pentecost, everybody understood. The word *tongues* is a Greek word
that should be translated "languages," for that is exactly what
they were and what the word literally means.

Scholars have come to differing conclusions as to what the
Pentecostal phenomenon was. One compelling view holds that
since everybody in the New Testament world spoke some variety
of Greek, that was, in various dialects, the language of the sermons. Whatever the experience, it was brought on when these
simple men, now apostles, who a month before had been hiding
out, were made bold and openly proclaimed Jesus as Lord and
Savior. The wind was blowing strongly, and these men of God had
hoisted their spiritual sails to catch it and to act. The original
author of this account was not so much concerned with what the
languages were, or how the apostles managed them, but with how
whatever went on revealed the power and presence of God.

Paul refers throughout his letters to the activity of the Spirit. Consistently the references are to the movement of God in the lives of Christians, and in the church. In 1 Corinthians 4, he lists specific gifts or abilities the Spirit gives to some Christians. Among these manifestations were: the utterance of wisdom, the utterance of knowledge, faith, gifts of healing, working miracles, prophecy, discernment, speaking languages (tongues), and the translation of languages (tongues). But remember, these gifts were always seen as having been given to the church, and were not just for anyone's personal edification.

The phenomenon of ecstatic languages—languages of heaven, emotionally charged sounds produced quite apart from any rational capacity—was a common part of the worship of other religious bodies in the ancient world. When one is caught up and overpowered by feelings, and ordinary worship or ordinary words cannot express the fullness of the moment, irrational sounds are often the result. If you have ever been to a football game when the home team scores a winning touchdown just as the final gun goes off, you will have noted that the sounds produced by the fans do not make much immediate sense.

Perhaps music is the most fundamental ecstatic utterance. Not everything is rational. There is the profundity of feelings in religion which needs to find expression, and therefore sentiments too deep for understandable words may be an appropriate vehicle for worship, publicly or in private.

This element of worship had obviously been adopted by some of Paul's churches, particularly at Corinth. While Paul admits to occasionally speaking in these "heavenly tongues," he downplays the phenomenon, claiming that he would rather speak a few understandable words than thousands in these peculiar emotionally charged, or heavenly, languages (1 Corinthians 14:18). Indeed, he claims that unless love dominates the speaker, both human languages and angelic tongues are useless noise (1 Corinthians 13:1).

The Fruits of the Spirit

Paul sees the work of the Spirit, as it blows through the lives of Christians, taking quite another legitimate shape. Those who are possessed by the Spirit begin to live differently. They begin to bear particular kinds of fruit— fruit of the Spirit. "Love, joy, peace, patience, kindness, generosity, faithfulness, gentleness, and self-control" (Galatians 5:22). These attributes, available to all Christians, are for Paul far more cogent evidences of the Spirit than the gifts that come to a few. Not everybody is emotionally or intellectually geared up to become driven to the point of ecstasy. But everyone can exhibit the fruit of the Spirit.

The parched religious ground upon which many modern liberal Christians walk has dried up among those who are not aware of and open to the Spirit. If the Spirit is the wind or breath of God, faith is to raise one's sails and move by its power. The hymn by Jessie Adams puts it this way:

I feel the winds of God today; today my sail I lift,
Tho' heavy oft with drenching spray, and torn by many
     a rift;
If hope but light the water's crest, and Christ my bark
     will use,
I'll seek the seas at his behest, and brave another cruise.

The excitement and adventure to which we are called by the power of God, happens when we are overwhelmed, and when we recognize the overwhelming as God active in our lives and in our midst. We call that activity and presence the Holy Spirit.

An ancient prayer asks for that presence:

Come Holy Spirit, come.
Come as the fire and burn.
Come as the wind and cleanse.
Come as the light and reveal.
Convict, convert, consecrate, until we are wholly thine.

In the previous three chapters we have discussed the three ways we experience the activity of God. If historically the names used were "Father, Son, and Holy Spirit," we have become aware that it has been difficult for modern people to understand God as a person, or three persons. But if we see God as energy and purpose—or energy with a purpose—we can get out from under a philosophic system that nobody today holds, and find a fresh vitality in our understanding of the three ways we experience the one God.

As we now proceed to other theological matters it will be helpful to occasionally reread these initial chapters, particularly when the going gets tough. They are the foundation stones upon which the rest must be built.

5

The Bible—
The Testimony of
God's People

No doubt many readers will already have raised questions about how today's theologians view the authority of the Bible. The Christian world seems deeply divided over this issue.

The Word of God

On one hand are the fundamentalists, and some evangelicals, who refer to the Bible as the Word of God, and by that designation assert that it contains the actual words of God. Not only in matters of religion, but in matters of history and science, they believe it to be true—literally true. Its truth flows from the inerrancy of its verbal inspiration. That is: God dictated the words directly to the person who wrote them down, and they are without error of any kind, or even the possibility of error. This is God speaking!

Despite what scientific research might reveal about the age of the earth or how long human beings have been around, for instance, if the Bible says that the whole enterprise is only six thousand years old, science is wrong. Every verse of Scripture is to be taken literally. You don't interpret the text, you just read it and realize that whatever it says is accurate in every detail. God is the author, and God doesn't make mistakes. The bumper sticker reads:

GOD SAID IT—I BELIEVE IT—THAT SETTLES IT

If significant numbers of layfolk are not getting that message from their own pastors, they are soaking it up from TV religion. In fact, these rigid absolutists, whose presence dominates religious programming, are about the only theological names known by significant numbers of today's layfolk. Most of those who occupy our pews couldn't name a single teacher in a single ecumenical or denominational seminary. Who are the principal interpreters of the gospel for them? Pat Robertson, James Dobson, and the others who spend and collect tens of millions of dollars annually to propagate their own form of American religion. And what they hold is not what is believed by the world's foremost biblical scholars, nor does it reflect the curricula of the world's finest seminaries—now or ever! Yet from the turn of the twentieth century the debate has raged, and the principal issue has been the role and authority of Scripture.

A Closed Book

On the other hand, there are many Christians today for whom the Bible is a closed book. They may read a few verses from time to time, or even regularly, but do not understand how it has authority for the Christian life. Countless numbers have been in adult Sunday school classes for decades. But too often Bible study has been limited to jumping up and down on ten verses every week and coming out of that social exercise just about where they went in. At best the Bible contains a collection of moralisms that one may or may not take seriously. Good old established adult Sunday school classes are precious to those who have found lifelong friendships there. But as vehicles for serious Bible study, many are ineffective.

For still others the Bible may be interesting literature, but outside a few selections, such as the Ten Commandments, how the Bible speaks authoritatively to the Christian, the church or the world is far from clear.

While the question of the authority of Scripture is important, it points to the larger issue: how does one know the truth, and what are the avenues for that knowledge? Or, is there any way to know the truth? Or, as Pilate said to Jesus, "What is truth?" In this chapter we will first consider the authority of the Scriptures, and then place that matter in the larger context of what constitutes authority for the Christian and for the church. What are the ways by which we both discern and know the will of God?

The Authority of the Scriptures

Let us now look at what the Bible is and how it came to us. With that discussion as background we will more intelligently be able to identify its authority.

While occasionally in Christian history devout followers have held the view that the Bible was indeed verbally inspired and is therefore inerrant, that has never been the prevailing view in the life of the church. It must be remembered that the church, immediately following Jesus, did not sit down with the New Testament and shape its life, thought, and doctrine using Scripture as a guide, but quite the opposite. The church produced the New Testament. The New Testament did not produce the church. There was no New Testament, as we know it, for centuries; only small collections of books in the hands of various churches. Some of the books in these collections were finally accepted as authoritative and some were not.

For a generation no written records were available. The more we know about how the Christian Scriptures came into being, the clearer we are about their relationship to an already thriving community of faith. Collections of writings, beginning with a few of Paul's letters, and later the synoptic Gospels— Matthew, Mark, and Luke—grew slowly. Various churches were in the possession of different sets of documents. And all of this after a period of time in which the stories of Jesus were circulated by word of mouth, only later to be written, gathered, and edited.

Even the issue of what books might be read in worship, the canon, was not settled for a very long time, and not finally nailed down until four hundred years after Jesus' death. The books selected, the twenty-seven we now have, were chosen because of their assumed ties with either apostles or those who were close to the apostles. Here were documents the church believed more clearly proclaimed God's saving acts in Jesus the Christ. It was believed that the church accepted particular books under the guidance of the Holy Spirit.

In those early centuries the church never believed they were handed down from heaven, or were divine. They could be trusted because they came from persons closest to the original events, and testified to what the early church otherwise believed about Jesus. Even the scribes, who in these early centuries and long after copied the documents by hand, did not believe they were dealing with inerrant texts. In fact, when they felt a correction was needed, a clarification called for or a contradiction cleared up, they first put the note in the margin, and the next generation of scribes often inserted it in the body of the text.

As time went on, it became clear that even to assemble an accurate Greek or Latin text was a matter of both painstaking research and some guesswork. The suggestion that God had dictated these materials and they were in any sense the word or words of God at their writing was never generally held. And even if the originals were divinely dictated, the point was moot since nobody had them, or anything short of manuscripts obtained from multiple generations of copying.

The problem gets even more difficult when we realize that to put together an original language text out of the multiplicity of differing manuscripts available was one thing, but to come up with an infallible translation was quite another. Since translation is not a "this word means that" exercise, but is largely an attempt to make sense out of linguistic idioms, it would take an infallible translator to get the words of God accurately to us.

The problem is even further complicated when you realize that culture produced the idiomatic verbal symbols that are subsequently put in written words, and culture is in a continual state of change. Words do not mean the the same thing from one generation to another. That is why every generation needs a fresh translation. The message may not change, but the language into which the message is put certainly does, just as does the philosophic worldview.

The same issues prevailed when religious leaders and scholars dealt with the Hebrew Scriptures. Just so people throughout the Jewish world could read them, great parts of what we have called the Old Testament were translated from Hebrew into the common language of the Mediterranean world: Greek.

Let us note at this point that from here onward we will refer to what is commonly called "The Old Testament" as "The Hebrew Scriptures." Since they were the product of an authentic pre-Christian community of faith, to call them "The Old Testament" presupposes an original organic relationship with "The New Testament." We will refer to the New Testament as "The Christian Scriptures," with the understanding that the "Old Testament" is also part of the Christian canon. To see both Hebrew and Christian Scriptures as having their own authenticity demands care in the designations we use.

With the Reformation, Protestantism developed a high view of biblical authority, even though the reformers were reluctant to assign inerrant authority to the twenty-seven books the earlier church had recognized as authoritative. Martin Luther declared that the book of James, for instance, was "an epistle of straw," and in one of his German versions put a blank page after Revelation, and then inserted James. So much for verbal inspiration!

The modern notion of an infallible book is really a late development birthed in the United States, growing out of eighteenth-century revivalism. As certain scholars and church leaders grew suspicious of the "modernism" rife in such radical institutions as Princeton University, and established their own Bible schools, the issue at the center of the controversy was biblical authority. The prevailing tradition viewed the texts as subject to literary evaluation and criticism. The question arose among these newly minted fundamentalists, "If one verse is in error, how can it be assumed that any verse is trustable?"

It was the need for certainty, in an age when both theories and information were exploding, that produced a retreat from critical procedures. Fundamentalists were suspicious of both the analysis of what wordings were authentic—lower criticism—and questions surrounding by whom and how documents came to be written in the first place—higher criticism. These scholarly exercises were seen as the effort of faithless liberals to call into question the authority of God's word.

There are other religions that see their sacred writings as just that—sacred. To this day followers of Islam believe that Allah dictated the Koran into the ear of the angel Gabriel, who then grasped the hand of the prophet Mohammot, who wrote it down word for word. For Muslims, the Koran is not only The Word of God, but The Words of God. Since Allah speaks only Arabic, and since any translation would corrupt the perfect text, there are no authorized translations of the Koran. To study it and know it requires that one speak and read Arabic.

If we view the Bible as a literary document that arose out of the faith of the community, and not from God's dictation, what is its authority? And furthermore, what about the claim that if the Bible is wrong at one point, how can we trust it at any point? Is it different than any other book, or is it subject to the errors of persons who were not infallible, who produced it and corrupted the text over centuries of copying, translating, and interpreting?

The Testimony of the People of God

If we are seeking to use the Bible as a collection of indexed verses to prove things, either about religion or about science or history, or if we see the Scriptures as accurate road maps into an already decided future, then there are no adequate answers to these questions, or even ways to explore them. But if we are open to seeing faith as a journey we make, using less than perfect resources, in response to a God who makes the journey with us, we can accept the Scriptures for what they are: testimonies of the people of God. The quest for absolute, final, definitive answers to that which is essentially a journey of faith—not of sight—is to ask for what is provable. However you define the Christian commitment, that is not what our sojourn with God is about.

How we view biblical authority must flow from how we understand the God that the Scriptures present. In the earlier chapters we viewed God as dynamic: intimately involved with us in nature and history. We have concluded that God is neither some far-off principal, nor a being as we are beings. God is that which underlies everything that is, who causes it, and who is the active agent in its existence. God is the verb of life—the doing, not just the doer. God is power with a purpose, and that purpose is continually breaking out in fresh generative ways, catching up someone here and some community there. We call that purpose "love." God is with us and in us, and we are in and with God. So God is not remote or simply other. Neither is "he" some distant being or set of principles.

God encounters us in the very processes of our lives and of the life of the world. One way we experience God's creative and purposeful energy is in Jesus, all of God we can experience in human form. And when we talk about how God interpenetrates our lives and our world day by day, we use the term *Holy Spirit*. God pro-acts and we participate in the redemptive process together with the faithful community—the church. Our experience with God can also be direct. We can be caught up in creative energy, in the love and loving relationships from whom all history comes, and toward which all existence moves. That is, God can be known, not only by us but by people in every generation who are attuned to the holy.

With that understanding of God, we can begin to make sense of the biblical message, how it was originally written and what authority it has today. From the dawn of our recorded history, persons and communities of persons, sensitive to what

God was about in the world, entered the flow of faith and with God became part of the redemptive enterprise. Looking at events that way has been called "holy history."

In the early days of human experience, how this got acted out may seem primitive to us. God was seen sometimes as a nature God, who needed to be appeased to make the crops grow or stop the storms. At other times God was seen as a tribal deity or military hero. God was later understood to be a commandment giver, and the religious life commandment keeping.

Later God was seen as the one who made covenant. God was perceived to have established a relationship with a particular group of people. Authentic religion was faithfulness to that covenant. Still later, others thought more clearly about the justice of God as it operated beyond their own tribe or system. Hope grew that people caught up in the divine flow would learn to live in harmony and equity, not only with those like themselves but also with others. Prophets, a designation that did not arise until many centuries after the Exodus, articulated this expanded notion of God and godly living.

As we look at religious history, none of these people and cultures had the whole truth. They did share, however, a growing sense of both the power and benevolence of God. Over the centuries our Hebrew foreparents acted together in communities of covenant. To clarify the record they began to write about their memories, tell stories, reflect on history and on the vital questions of existence. These stories were subsequently collected, edited, and reshaped, and later emerged as religious documents.

Among our Jewish foreparents these writings finally were formed into various collections, which began to be widely read and accepted. From a vast number of verbal stories, and then writings, people of faith began to select those which they believed more clearly told the truth about their history and how their faithful ancestors saw God active in it. Some of these writings achieved a status beyond others, because they seemed to capture the heart of the testimonies of faith and of witness. Slowly canons, or lists of writings, were assembled, and these became, by the decision of a number of faithful bodies, holy or set aside. Instead of thinking of them coming down from above, we now know they were generated out of the lives, experiences, and encounters of the people of God.

The list of those books considered to be more reliable did not appear all at once. As with the Christian Scriptures, which took the church four hundred years to distill and define, the official canon of Hebrew Scriptures grew and matured over long periods of time. These books, said the communities of faith, were authored by those most under the sway of God's Spirit. Here were the products of writers, collectors, and editors most in tune with the winds of God, into whom God breathed more clearly. In other words, here were the products of inspired— "breathed into"—men and women. It is not that *writings* were inspired, but that *writers* were. Here were the documents that told of encounters men and women of old had with God. Here were the reliable testimonies of the people of God. They could be trusted, not as science, but as testaments of faith.

When they were read, they were not assumed to be the Words of God, but words of people through whom the Spirit of God blew. Nevertheless, all written documents were and are subject to the science, perspectives, points of view, political realities, literary rules, historical limitations and philosophic frameworks of those who did the writing, collecting, and editing. One must always read ancient texts in light of the people who produced them—who they were, what their world looked like, what philosophic systems determined how they viewed things, what was going on politically, what their scientific understanding was, and so on. Here are the writings of those thought to be closest to God, in whom and through whom God worked.

The Scriptures, therefore, can be trusted to tell the truth about those testimonies, those people, and their experiences. Sometimes they described their encounters with God by means of stories, fables, poetry, and the great mythic sagas that developed and were told and retold for hundreds of years before being put in the written form we now have.

The church chose the twenty-seven books in our Christian canon because they were testimonies to Jesus and to the experiences of Jesus' earliest followers, the reliable witnesses. Beyond that, it was held that these books testified to the gospel—the unmerited love of God. Nevertheless, rarely in church history was it believed that every verse had equal authority. Their authority grew out of how they reflected the gospel, not the other way around.

The Scriptures, therefore, Hebrew and Christian, must be read not as books of science or history, but as testimonies of faith. Thus understood they are normative, bearing authoritative testimony to the experiences people had with the vital force of life and existence we call God. The Bible is, therefore, the foundation stone of authority for the Christian life and for the life of the Christian community. It was produced by Spirit-led people, and forms the framework for our faith. It is not just a book beside other books. But it did not come down from heaven. It came up out of the experiences of God's people as they felt the winds of the Spirit blow through their lives.

If then the Scriptures are authoritative for the Christian and for the church, are they the only way to know the truth? Common sense tells us that we know the truth in a variety of ways. You may tell me something I did not know before and which has never been written in the Bible or elsewhere. I may discover something I had not previously understood in a course in physics or history. I may arrive at some fresh insight as I think through an issue on my own. In fact, there are a great variety of ways we form conclusions as to what is true.

The Great Conversation—with Others

If our knowledge of God and of the world in which God is intimately involved comes first of all from the testimony of ancient reliable witnesses, that evidence must always be tested against other resources and voices. It is as we stay in conversation with a multiplicity of voices that we discern not only what is true, but what is right and good and holy. I call the way we receive and analyze all these data, "the great conversation."

Most of the voices with which we converse are outside ourselves. We need name but a few. We listen not only to Scripture but also to Christians who have lived since the church closed the canon—and before. If God spoke through faithful witnesses of old, as the Spirit blew through their lives, why should we assume that when the last bit of Christian Scripture was penned God signed off?

God has spoken and continues to speak through the church. Catholics have a better handle on this way to know the truth than do many Protestants. Catholics speak of the Tradition, which is a way to describe the activity of God century after century. We know the truth, therefore, by knowing church history. Our fathers and mothers in the faith are part of the community with whom we must stay in continual dialogue. Saints, martyrs, poets, priests, monks, prophets, servants of the poor, scholars, and multitudes of others all share in the great conversation.

But aren't there voices outside our faith tradition that also help inform us? All of history is there for our enlightenment. Secular leaders and common people, both in Europe and the United States, and in places unknown to the West for most of Western history, have much for us to learn and understand. We include them in the conversation. There are scientists, linguists, poets, philosophers and yes, even politicians, with whom we must be in conversation! Indeed, the whole field of human knowledge becomes a resource and a partner.

And what about those of other religions or of no religion? And doesn't nature itself add to our store of knowledge and of faith? "The heavens are telling the glory of God; and the firmament proclaims [God's] handiwork" (Psalm 19:1). The more we know about the universe, the more we know about the God who is the energy by which it all has been given being.

There are yet other external voices. Every reader of this book has something to teach me if only we were in communication.

Add to that the hundreds of people whose paths I cross, everyone of whom has information that might enrich my store of what is so, and what is right and good.

All of these sources are outside ourselves. As we converse with the Bible we also converse with these other voices, and in doing so the Bible is open to us in new and vital ways. In the same manner, as we deal with the Bible, every conversation with the other external voices enriches who we are and enlarges what we know about God.

The Great Conversation—with the Self

If there are external ways of knowing, there are also voices that come from within. As we find ourselves caught up by the Spirit of God, we often intuitively know what is right and what is true. Most of the time the messages of these inner sources are generated somewhere along the line from one or more of the partners in our external conversations. But there are those occasions when nothing from the outside provides any definitive answer. Occasionally, having sifted through all the evidence, we arrive at a conclusion that seems to defy the external evidence. There are some things I know to be true I cannot prove by citing any authority, except that is what I believe.

The affections are occasionally self-validating. Love often defies the evidence or the rational. Or consider what is commonly called conscience. We have all had occasions when we did not know what to do or believe, and through the inner disciplines of prayer, introspection or meditation we arrived at a conclusion. Our spirits intersect with and are interpenetrated by the Spirit of God. Abraham left Ur to seek a land he was to receive as an inheritance, not even knowing where he was to go. Despite all the external evidence, he responded to a call nobody else seemed to hear.

Many new discoveries come about when someone takes a leap of faith, putting into the equation a piece of fresh information that seems to come from the depths of the human spirit or mind.

While these internal voices are to be taken seriously, most of the time they must be validated by one of more of the external sources. Seldom can we trust them by themselves. If the voice of conscience tells me to shoot my child, chances are it is some emotional disturbance, not divinely led conscience, which is providing the direction. The internal voices are of the greatest authority only when they participate and are tested and weighed in the rest of the great conversation.

Whether we are listening to the internal or the external evidence, we begin to discover the truth when we find more and more of the voices in the conversation in agreement. For thoughtful people, there arises a consensus in which one voice says "yes" to other voices. And ultimately we are wise to test out even these preliminary conclusions against the authority of Scripture.

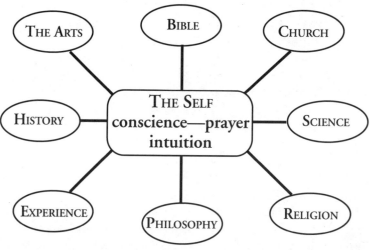

Paul Tillich referred to the external authorities as "heteronomous"—from two Greek words, *heteros,* meaning other, and *nomos,* meaning law. Put them together and you get "law from the other." Danger arises when the law of the other is limited to evidence coming from just a few voices— or just one! The sound of a single external voice that makes an absolute claim to truth spells tyranny.

On the other hand, the word for "law of the self" is even more familiar: *autonomy. autos*—"self" and *nomos*— "law." Rarely is anyone or any church a law in itself. There can also be the tyranny of my opinion, or my congregation's. More mischief, inside and outside the Christian community, has been produced by people who assumed they were the final authority on everything. Yet there are times when having sifted all the evidence, I must decide not only what is true but what course of action best reflects the will of God. I always appreciated the chap who said, "I don't know what I'm going to do, but *I'm* going to do it."

God—the Final Authority

Ultimately it is God who is the final authority in the life of the Christian and in the life of the church. Tillich calls this ultimate authority "theonomous": *Theos*—"God" and *autos*— "self." But the question remains: If God is the final authority, how do we know what God's will is? We have answered that question by suggesting the far-reaching dialogue called the great conversation. We judge what the will of God is for any given moment or set of circumstances in the context of this diverse listening and speaking.

While Scripture may be the most substantial voice in the mix, we are on thin ice if we think that a verse of scripture settles anything. I have often offered the following wager: recite any doctrine of faith, no matter how sound or how absurd, and I will find a Bible verse that proves it and a Bible verse that disproves it. We are called to share in the great adventure of faith. We must do so without the absolute proof that comes from a book, a law, an institution, or even the self.

6

The Cross and
Our Salvation

Central to the Christian faith is the affirmation that Christ's death on the cross saves us. How this is accomplished, or even what it means, has occupied the minds and hearts of the faithful since the first Christian century. Ever since Paul affirmed that God was in Christ reconciling the world to Godself (2 Corinthians 5:19), the discussion has spawned a plethora of terms each of which has been the subject of enormous amounts of theological inquiry.

Grace, hope, love—and their doctrinal derivatives: justification, redemption, sacrifice, atonement, ransom, substitution, lamb of God—are but a few of the images that have occupied the best minds in the long history of the church. To attempt a definition of one of these terms would take a library. And even with these definitions we still might not be any closer to answering the question at the root of them all: How does the death of Christ save us?

Salvation

Of all the complex terms, none is more difficult than the seemingly simple word *save*. What does it mean to be saved?

Saved from what? Saved to what? Saved for what? Saved by what? Can you feel coming on a four-pronged sermon, each of whose points is a pinprick on a universe of complexity? Perhaps the word is best understood when it is stripped of the accretions that over the centuries have fastened themselves to it like barnacles on the hull of a ship.

The basic meaning of the Greek word we translate *saved*, is to be whole or healed. The word itself has nothing to do with heaven, getting rid of sins, being made right with God, joining the church, making a confession of faith, receiving baptism, or arriving at some level of Christian perfection. Rather it has to do with healing that which is broken. Reduced to a modern colloquialism we could say that saved means "getting it all put together." For Christians this is not an act we perform. It is a gift of God to which we respond in faith.

If something has come apart and is mended, the word used in secular as well as in sacred literature is *saved*. A disease conquered would merit the same term. To be in a complete, whole, healthy state, therefore, is to be saved. To restore a broken relationship is to save it. "Wholeness" is a better entree to the meaning of the word than is "rescue." Yet, the word is so broad it is easy to see how almost anyone with any point of view, from escaping hell to healing a skin rash, has been able to claim the concept. But having defined it, that still does not tell us how the death of Christ does the trick, or even what the trick is.

Broken and Separated

Perhaps the best place to begin is by thinking about what is broken, in need of healing, or unwholesome. The Hebrew myths, recorded in the first chapters of Genesis, make it clear that something went wrong. Jewish religionists, who told and later recorded and refined the stories, knew that life was fractured and grim. Simple observation drew the obvious conclusion that people didn't get along with each other, had to fight a hostile earth just to survive, had a terrible problem with their individual identities, and had lost contact with God.

Eden's story told how originally everything stood in right relationship to everything else. Adam and Eve were content and happy in Eden. The earth was friendly. God saw that everything that had been created was good. And then it all fell apart— literally. Things got broken. Our first mythical parents were naked and ashamed. They hid from God, having lost confidence in who they were. They were at enmity with each other, blaming and disputing. And in the next generation it came to murder! The physical world was no longer friendly. Eden was closed, not just closed for repairs, but permanently closed! And God? A great gulf now existed between humankind and the Creator. It is easy to understand how the doctrine of original sin developed. Just look around! If we were not born in sin we have taken to it with considerable gusto. Our world is essentially broken, not just out of adjustment.

Thus the human situation seemed fractured four ways: with self, others, nature, and God. While Eden's perfection doubtless never existed, most cultures have had a nostalgia for a perfect but lost world. Remember, Jews have traditionally illumined reality by telling stories, and the Genesis account is an edited compilation of a number of Hebrew myths. A myth is not a fictional, made-up fairy tale. It is an effort by a culture to offer, in story form, answers to the most profound questions of human life: Where did we come from? Who were our forebears? Why is life so hard? Why is there suffering and death? No one doubted then, or now, that something was broken, and that the brokenness was deeply rooted in the experience of Earth's most ancient people.

In the accounts of holy history God gets to work immediately to heal the trouble, and that saga dominates the biblical message. God does it through a people, a law, a covenant, a land, a tradition, and a hope. The Hebrew Scriptures are an extended record of how people perceived God at work, attempting to overcome the rift. Was God unsuccessful? Things at the end of two thousand years of Hebrew history were not much better than they had been at the beginning. In fact, the human condition seemed to be built on the sinking sands of separation and alienation.

God the Reconciler

The meaning of salvation, therefore, must be related to ways in which God has been at work to overcome the separation and reunite that which had been torn apart. The Christian story focuses this activity of God, working with power and with purpose, through and in Jesus. The focal point of this activity is the cross. Perhaps the best shorthand way to express it is in the text cited at the beginning of this chapter. "In Christ God was reconciling the world to [Godself]" (2 Corinthians 5:19).

The story of the cross is rooted in God's effort to reunite that which is separated and to heal the brokenness. If, as we indicated earlier, the word *saved* means to make whole or to mend, we can begin to see the relationship between the cross and salvation.

How we understand God's saving activity in the cross of Christ depends, as do most things in Christian theology, on our understanding of God. In fact, every theory produced to make sense of how the cross saves us is conditioned by the way in which the theorists view God. This may be one of those points when a review of Chapter Two, about God, might be helpful.

If one's notion of God is (1) as a being, a great deity who lives in the sky and who may be powerful, but not *that* powerful, an antagonist inevitably enters the drama. This is particularly true for those who traditionally see God as pure light, and the darkness of creation in the hands and under the control of a lesser god who is easily turned into a personification of evil—the devil. While not quite a belief in two gods, the notion that God had a powerful adversary got into the Hebrew tradition several hundred years before the Christian era, through the Persians. These neighbors believed that some lesser being created and controlled this physical world, and that God dwelt in an unapproachable light. How else could they explain the evil that abounded? God had to compete with a demonic force, and it was a hard battle with an uncertain outcome.

If God is understood (2) as a divine sovereign, a king—to use a political term, or a lord—to use a feudal term, then how one views the cross flows from that understanding. It was the king or lord's honor that was at stake. If the king is insulted somebody must pay for it.

If God is seen (3) as a benevolent and forgiving father, who wants us to live gracious lives and sets the example, then yet another notion of the cross takes center stage. Indeed, it was these three notions of God that generated the most common early theories about how the cross saves.

The Ransom Theory

(1) Consider a worldview in which God is not in charge. Some lesser evil authority is in charge. Call this being Satan, or the devil, or the prince of darkness. This demonic presence, so goes the theory, not only owns the earth but has also taken control of the souls of all humankind. He got them when we, through Adam and Eve, fell for his deceit, and sinned. Now owning us lock, stock, and barrel, there is no way we can extricate ourselves from his grasp. God, who is remote from our experience but looks with pity, sees our plight and decides to pay off the devil. What is the amount of the ransom? Far more than we could ever raise. There is only one thing good enough to secure our freedom: the blood of God's own son. God pays up. Jesus dies as a blood sacrifice—a ransom delivered to the devil. And we are set free.

> There was none other good enough to pay the price for
> sin.
> He only could unlock the gate of heaven, and let us in.

This effort to explain how the death of Christ saves us—in this case from the devil's dominion—is called the ransom theory. It rests on a very strange, archaic notion of God. Be that as it may be, the ransom theory hangs around even today. As is the case with every theological proposition under the sun—good or silly—there are Bible verses, which if taken out of context, are used in support. In Matthew 20:28 Jesus says that he came to serve and "to give his life [as] a ransom for many." And the writer of 1 Timothy 2:6 holds that "Christ Jesus…gave himself [as] a ransom for all." While these metaphoric verses do not lay out a definitive notion of what the ransom was all about and to whom it was paid, they were enough to stimulate later theologians into constructing the theory described here.

Note the direction of the action in this theory. The one toward whom the action flows is the devil. It is his terms that must be satisfied. He must be paid off. God yields, antes up, and we are thankful bystanders. God may love us, but God doesn't own us, nor is God able to act without mollifying the antagonist.

The Substitutionary Theory

(2) If one's notion of God, however, is as a king or a lord, whose honor is at stake, then another theory of how the cross saves us comes into play. This regal being cannot tolerate sin. Sin offends his dignity. And again our sinfulness, inherited from our earliest foreparents, traps us all. Because God is outraged, somebody must pay the penalty so that his subjects can again live in harmony with their sovereign. The subjects—that's us—may try to raise the bounty. But it is hopeless. There is not enough goodness or wealth in the whole world to satisfy the divine judgment. And not posting the fine, we are about to get what we deserve—damnation, death, and hell. At the last minute, however, Christ enters the scene and just before we are hauled to the gallows, he takes our place, a voluntary substitute. For God, the death of his perfect, pure, sinless son is good enough. Jesus dies, God is paid off in Jesus' blood and we are forgiven—saved. From what are we saved? From a divine wrath that demands the death penalty, and will settle for nothing short of our blood—or the blood of Jesus.

That is such a horrible iniquitous image of God, it is difficult for many of us to understand how any thinking Christian could have considered it. Yet the substitutionary theory of the atonement has been around for a long time, and has received renewed currency in modern fundamentalism.

The notion that "Christ died in my place" is very much part of our religious folklore. Put that way the theory has a certain almost sentimental appeal. But when it is examined, the notion of God on which it rests is appalling.

This theory makes no sense apart from a regal or feudal deity. If in the ransom theory the action was done for the sake of the devil, who was paid off, in the substitutionary theory the direction of the action is toward God. Jesus pays the debt, and God's honor is satisfied. We are again thankful bystanders. It is God who must be appeased. As crude as it seems, that is what you end up with when God is a royal personage.

The Moral Influence Theory

(3) Some theologians of the Middle Ages, reacting to these theories, viewed God, and thus salvation, in quite another way. God was neither a remote person up there somewhere, paying off the devil, who really ran things, nor was God a royal or feudal personage, whose honor had to be vindicated. God was a loving parent who wanted us to be reconciled, and knew that on our own we could never find our way out of our self-imposed separation and sinfulness.

Over the centuries God tried everything, and nothing worked. But since it is God's nature to love and to give, God decides to set an example. God sends us Jesus. He teaches us that God is love and that to be in right relationship to God means to love God and to love each other. But we still fail to understand. Jesus' teaching ministry is helpful, but it is not enough.

In one last great demonstration produced to show us what love means, Jesus dies by our hands and on account of our sinfulness. And God, instead of condemning us for the crime, forgives us. The hope is that seeing the example of love in action, we are converted, brought back to God, taught to make better decisions, and are reconciled. The death of Christ saves us only insofar as it is an object lesson to which we respond. It is the moral influence, for that is what the theory was called, which brings us back into right relationship with God—or at least provides the opportunity. In this theory we are saved from our proclivity to make bad self-damning decisions. In the final analysis, the moral influence theory holds that it is our action that reconciles us to God. We respond to Jesus' example and turn home again.

This theory solved a few of the nastier problems inherent in the ransom theory and the substitutionary theory. God is neither a bumbling, helpless, remote person, who has to pay off the devil, nor is God an aristocrat, who must be pampered and appeased. God is a loving parent, or perhaps a benevolent grandparent, who sets an example, hoping we will catch on. The act is directed toward us. The death is not for the devil's sake nor for God's sake, but for our sakes. Nevertheless, in the moral influence theory God is still remote, still acting outside our experience, still an independent agent.

While all three of the above theories have some biblical base and have been variously popular in Christian history, consider how the cross takes on a whole different meaning under the definition of God suggested in Chapter Two.

God the Reconciler

To review briefly:

The only way we can know God or anything about God is when we experience God in our midst. If God acts beyond our experience, we are left with only conjecture. Humbly we admit that we who are finite can never solve the Mystery that is God. It is always beyond our deepest thought.

Yet the Scriptures, history, and nature all testify to a God who is very much with us. We have defined God as power with a purpose. Not only is God the Creator and Sustainer—nouns, but God is the creating and sustaining—verbs! The very process of life, every breath we take is by God's Spirit. No, God is not the creation. God is the creative energy that enlivens everything. God doesn't "be"—that is, God is not an item, an object, a being. It is the *doing* we call God.

This dynamic and energized notion of God does not leave us with an ethically neutral set of propositions. The doing is all for a purpose. We call that purpose by the simplest of names: love. There is a direction to the doing and to the creation in which the doing is active. The tiniest seed may appear brown and inert, but there is built into that seed a purpose, and the seed struggles, sometimes up through concrete, to fulfill that purpose. We who are creatures of the earth have the remarkable capacity to cooperate with that seed, to prepare the soil, do the planting, watering, and cultivating.

Just so, God is the ultimate or total purpose of life. And that purpose moves inextricably toward the goal for which creation exists. We not only understand that purpose, we can participate in its happening. And what is the purpose? It is to bring everything into harmony, to reconcile the world to Godself. Every page of Christian Scripture testifies to that purpose. God loved the world. God wills that the world and all that is in it be reconciled to Godself. All creation eagerly awaits this reconciliation (Romans 8:19–23). And the purpose is performed among us, through us and in us.

The way we are most profoundly encountered by this purpose is through Jesus the Christ. God not only loved the world, but "so loved the world that he gave his only Son, so that everyone who believes in him may not perish but may have eternal life" (John 3:16). That is, it is the purpose of God that we and all creation be made whole, or *saved!* "In Christ God was reconciling the world to [Godself]" (2 Corinthians 5:19).

Paul goes to the heart of his theology in a letter to the Colossians. When describing the work of Jesus the Christ, he says, "For in him all the fullness of God was pleased to dwell, and through him God was pleased to reconcile to himself all things, whether on earth or in heaven, by making peace through the blood of his cross" (Colossians 1:19).

God's love—the purpose of this power—is to reconcile all things, to bring back into harmony that which has been broken. In other words, to save! And that is accomplished by the cross.

What we have here is not only an *active* God, but a God who is *activity*, not just the machine but the energy, the motion, the life force that makes a machine a machine and not just a pile of metal. This power with a purpose acts in the world, has a will for it, and is continually at work to bring everything back into harmony. To think of God as all-knowing or all-powerful makes of God a being, outside and remote. To think of God as that which reconciles and the reconciling itself, puts God right in our midst, the force that motivates our lives, the life of the world and all things, visible and invisible. The way we most clearly experience "God with us" is in Jesus. And the central sign of God being with us is the cross. God in Jesus not only suffers, but suffers with us, as one of us.

To understand God in this way, instead of a remote being who had to pay off the devil for our souls, a king whose honor had to be satisfied, or a teacher who offered a dramatic object lesson, allows us to see with new eyes how the cross saves us. We are saved as Jesus, who is all of God we can experience in human form, enters our experience and suffers with us and for us—even to death. God is not some obscure principle. God becomes the heartbreak of the world, a suffering we know because it is our experience too.

In the cross of Jesus the Christ we have God, who has become so much a part of our experience, that all the risks of living have fallen on his shoulders. The cross is God's act, not just an example, not just a transaction, but the actual experience of what goes on in our broken world. We know that nothing happens for good without somebody suffering. And we are bonded to this one, whose tears are shed and whose blood is poured out in solidarity with our broken hearts, spirits, and lives.

Note the direction of the action. It is not toward the devil. It is not back toward God. It is not even toward us—it is not an object lesson. It has its own authenticity. It is God in Jesus the Christ participating with us in our tragedy and sinfulness. And in the vortex of suffering love we find hope and are brought back into a right relationship with ourselves, one another and God. As God identifies with us in the cross we are reconciled. In the community of those who hurt, we are made whole, *saved!*

All the complexity of our experience is focused at the cross. When we say that he died for our sins, we mean that he died as a result of our sins, and the sinfulness of all humankind. Jealousy, greed, political manipulation, self-will, arrogance, and all the other things of which we are guilty produced the cross. It is not that the cross provides a bridge to God's happy, light-filled domain, but that God participates in the tragedy that is part of the human condition. And in the crucible of pain we are reconciled, reunited, and made whole.

Sin is more than a collection of our mistakes. It is the world's condition. In the cross God, through Christ, identifies with this brokenness, suffers on its account, and takes upon Godself the results. God is not remote—not some objective reality. God cannot be separated from the world's despair and brokenness. God's journey is not apart from our journey. The cross is the pivotal metaphor that describes God's identification with us and our troubled world. As such it is a sign of hope. God is with us!

Grace

If we see the cross that way, flowing from an understanding of God, who is the life force and through whom all things are given meaning, the difficult words listed at the beginning of this chapter can be either understood or put aside. The first word in that list, however, demands our attention. It is *grace*. Together with *love*, *grace* may be the most profound and important word in the Christian vocabulary. It reminds us that all of this divine activity is by God's initiative—the outcome of what power with a purpose is all about. We did not conjure it, produce it, deserve it, demand it, expect it, or earn it. It is simply the activity of God whose overriding will and purpose it is to reconcile the world to Godself. It is the way love works. *Grace* wraps up the entire divine initiative in a single word. The whole content of the Christian life, therefore, becomes a response to God in Jesus the Christ, reconciling the world to Godself by the blood of the cross.

And we are compelled to respond:

Were the whole realm of nature mine,
That were a present far too small.
Love, so amazing, so divine
Demands my life, my soul, my all.

7

Suffering, Evil—
And a God of Goodness

The most difficult and persistent problem in Christian theology has been the question of suffering and evil. Every year another shelf of books is produced attempting to explain why the world is infected with unimaginable pain. The brightest answers seem to stick around as long as the latest rock tune, and then another spate of authors take a crack at fathoming why a good and powerful God and horrendous evil can exist side by side. A school of Greek philosophers many centuries ago put the dilemma this way:

> God is all-powerful and all-loving.
> An all-powerful God would be able to prevent evil.
> An all-loving God would want to prevent evil.
> But evil exists
> Therefore, there is no God.

Free Will and "Original Sin"

The easy solutions to this logical dilemma have all turned out to be non-answers or answers that leave major questions unattended. Perhaps the most acceptable among the traditional responses has been the notion that when God gave humankind free will, God stepped back from being coercively powerful. Indeed, the abdication of authority was just another sign of God's power. God's power is seen even in God's decision not to exercise it! Please don't try and run that one through your logical system. It is an argument from silence, without evidence. It relies on the assumption that humans have free will, at least in some things, and therefore God, respecting that gift, has chosen not to interfere.

Other thinkers have attacked the problem by pointing out that sin has its consequences, and that when our original parents ate the wrong apple, evil was the result. Obviously many terrible things are produced by our wrong decisions. Anyone who believes that our actions do not produce fairly predictable results doesn't live in the same world I do. Smoke cigarettes for forty years and you run a great risk of ending up with cancer or heart disease. Produce an economic system based on much for the few and little for the many and you will have, first, enormous poverty, and, ultimately, revolution.

But how does free will or the notion that evil deeds produce evil consequences explain an earthquake or a tornado? It seems rather an enormous logical leap to assert that when human beings fell from favor with God by their own actions, all nature was thereby corrupted. Often coupled with that notion is the proposition that God is not all-powerful, and that the devil, the personification of evil, really owns and may have even created the natural world. Since we are children of the devil, we deserve whatever happens. Evil is what we've got coming.

Some Other Answers

There are others who believe there is no such thing as evil, and what we call evil is only goodness in a form we do not understand. Tell that to a mother who has just watched her child die of a rare viral infection.

Then there have always been religious people around who believe that what we call evil is overcome if only we have enough faith. "All things are possible, only believe."

When my 25-year-old son was killed in an airplane accident, a very pious young man told me that I could have prayed over the ashes of his body—which was all that remained—and brought him back to life. The problem was not in the accident but in my lack of faith.

And then there are the comforters who tell the afflicted that God is testing them. Or what about the idea that evil is only a temporary setback because all shall be well in heaven, which is the end product of the Christian life to begin with? So why worry about earthly troubles? As I suggested earlier, there are Bible verses to back up all of these theories, and Bible verses to knock each one down.

These and a score of other attempts to resolve the problem of evil have appeared from time to time, not only in Christian history, but in almost every culture. Reread the book of Job and you will discover that the three comforters, who tried to explain to Job why he had been devastated by one calamity after another, pretty much ran the gamut of the traditional answers. None of their attempts satisfied Job, and none of the answers generally given satisfy most of us. But then Job's quiet acceptance of the will of God doesn't satisfy us either. "The LORD gave and the LORD has taken away; blessed be the name of the LORD" (Job 1:21b), while intoned at many a graveside, leaves an empty place in most of our hearts.

And, of course, the very worst thing you can say to parents who have just seen their child die is, "God just wanted little Sarah more than you did." What kind of a nasty, selfish, bestial God is that?!

Now let us look at what underlies these unsatisfying answers. On what sort of theological base are they built? As has been our point of view throughout this book, how we understand God will determine how we respond to practically every other theological question. The way we view the question of evil, therefore, flows from what we mean by God.

Most of the answers suggested above presuppose a certain image of God; a being, an entity with a personality as we have personalities. We have used the masculine pronoun "he" throughout this chapter thus far, not because we are insensitive to questions of inclusive language, but because when God is imaged as King or Lord a feeling of masculinity automatically adheres. It is this male-dominated symbolic language that further reinforces notions of hierarchy and domination. That's what kings and lords are like.

Not All-Loving?

Once we accept a traditional definition, which makes God a person or a being—here you may want to look again at Chapter Two—we are inescapably impaled on the horns of the dilemma quoted at the beginning of this chapter. The initial major premise, "An all-powerful God would be able to prevent evil," leads us to one conclusion. Think carefully about the kind of all-powerful God we are describing. We edge toward the notion of a sovereign Lord, who may not be all that concerned, let alone loving. God can do what he pleases, he just doesn't desire to prevent our suffering.

Thus conceived we have a mighty miracle worker in the skies, who although he can do whatever he wants to, doesn't care to be of much help. If God wants to take away the viral infection devastating the body of that little baby, he can. And, in fact, all of us will probably pray that he does exactly that. And when the baby dies, the logical conclusion must be that God didn't choose to intervene. God, therefore, is not as loving as any ordinary physician, let alone any half-decent father, either of whom would move heaven and earth to save that child. How could any all-powerful deity sit by passively and watch six million of his chosen people die in Hitler's gas chambers? Or is it that God was just disinterested—with the power but not with the will?

Not All-Powerful

Or, if we take the other horn of the dilemma, God is loving all right, but never had, or perhaps lost, or gave away the ability to get things done. Our notion of God then is reduced to a benevolent fuddy-duddy, who may will the good but can't effect it. When it comes to things earthly or physical, God comes out second-best to the devil, who can accomplish the malevolent deeds he sets out to do.

What will you have for your heavenly deity; a powerful King who is unconcerned, or a loving Father who is ineffective? Well, if God is seen as a being, a person, you are hung with one or the other.

The Unsolved Dilemma

What about the evidence, usually anecdotal, about all the times God did intervene on behalf of someone, and they were healed or raised from the dead or cleansed of a demon? What about all the mighty works recorded in the Gospels? What about God causing the sun to stand still so Joshua could finish a slaughter? Well, if God is that powerful, why wasn't he powerful enough to stop the slaughter in the first place and simply declare that everybody live together peacefully? Is it becoming clear that the deeper you get into this pit, the stickier the mud?

Or consider the crash of a commercial airliner carrying two hundred people. One hundred of them are killed and the other hundred are not. Somebody among the hundred who survived, or one of their relatives, will credit prayer and faith for the miracle. Does anyone really suppose that the good, faithful, praying Christians all sat in the tail of the plane, which broke off and was not engulfed in flames, thereby allowing their survival, while the non-praying infidels all sat in the front of the plane, which exploded?

Perhaps the cleanest answer is to suggest that any answer is beyond us, but that we should pray for miracles nevertheless. That may be our best alternative as long as we hold onto a concept of God that makes of him a superperson, who can do whatever he pleases.

God in Our Midst

Consider, however, a very different notion of God. We might look at the question of evil with new eyes if we are not dealing either with a grand King or a benevolent Father in the sky, or any similar notion of deity. What if, as we suggested in Chapter Two, God is not a big, bright, powerful person at all? What if God is the force, the energy, that gives everything being, purpose, and meaning? What if, instead of being out there somewhere, God is intimately involved with us in everything we do and are? And what if God struggles with us, suffers with us, shares our lot—good and ill? Certainly "God-with-us" is at the heart of the Christian message.

Consider God as power with a purpose, the creative life force at the root of everything. And consider that this God is working with us and with all creation and all history. God struggles with us, not as an outsider but as the purposeful energy who shares our journey toward the "omega point," that goal of history that the Christian Scriptures call "the reign of God." If all history and all creation are still in process, and we have not arrived at the culmination of the adventure, then both God and the rest of us walk together along a common road.

Understood this way, neither creation nor human history is complete. They are both still in the making. According to the Genesis myths, the creation took time—six days or epochs. Instead of creation being the bringing of something out of nothing, what if creation is bringing order out of chaos over long, epochal periods? To the extent that there is still chaos, what we call evil, creation is not yet complete—it is still going on.

Considering that the universe is expanding in every direction all the time at the speed of light, could it be that we might still be in the early morning of the sixth day? If we know from geological and other scientific endeavors that the epochs of creative time were enormously long—billions and billions of years—and that human beings have been on this earth but a few tens of thousands, it is entirely possible that we are nearer the beginning than the end of the human enterprise. Whatever value lies in the theories of evolution, we know that higher forms of life continue to develop from lower forms of life. There is nothing finished or final about our history or our universe. In fact, it may never be finished, if finished means perfect and complete. We are always on the way, and the creative process is never-ending.

Nature is very fragile. What we identify as evil, therefore, is a reflection of the incompleteness of creation. Indeed, the very nature of creation involves chance, an ongoing process, not a finely tuned perfect, unbreakable machine. Nature is dynamic, not static, and wherever there is dynamism there is the possibility of a variety of outcomes, some good, some not so good—at least as we identify good. Of course, that is a very partial answer, an attempt to factor into the equation what cannot be explained by human sin.

Now reflect back on how this notion is linked to a dynamic concept of God—power with a purpose—a God who is still at work within the natural as well as the historic order—God with us.

It should be noted that this is not the same liberal theory which took evolutionary concepts and deduced that the world, including humankind, was on a social escalator, and that every day in every way things were getting better and better. Humankind is not getting appreciably better. If we ever thought that, two world wars, the Holocaust, Hiroshima, and the indescribable destruction going on every day at the hands of even the best of us shatters the naive assumption. Yet if humankind is not slowly moving toward some sort of perfection, that does not deny the generative power of God, who is always at work to bring order out of chaos, sometimes with our cooperation and sometimes in spite of our arrogance and proclivity to do the wrong thing.

Consider how the Christian gospel fits within this understanding of God. If Jesus is all of God we can see and know in human form, it becomes clear why the heart of the gospel is the cross—the sign not only of God's love but of God's suffering love; right here in our midst! In the Christian story, Jesus enters our history, not as some outside superperson, but as one of us. He shares our common lot, lives out the love that is at the heart and purpose of God's relationship to the world, and dies on account of the evil, which is not a matter of some divine play at smoke and mirrors, but very real and profoundly related to the human experience.

Perhaps a story can sum it up. Once a woman was having a very difficult time. Her world had fallen apart. Her child had died, her husband had left her, her health was broken. She was a writer, but would spend hour after hour staring blankly at her equally blank computer screen. She had come to the point where she believed that the only way out was to take her own life. In a quandary as to how to accomplish her demise, she walked the streets of her city seeking a solution that would be quick, painless, and final. But nothing occurred to her. She was too afraid to jump from a building or throw herself in front of a truck, and she had neither pills nor a lethal weapon. Late in the afternoon, bone tired, she decided to rest for a while on a cushioned pew in a Catholic church, which was open to the street. As she sat there weeping, she happened to look up and saw suspended over an altar the image of a man hanging on a cross, blood running from hands, feet and side; a crown of thorns piercing his head. And he too was weeping. It occurred to her that, whoever he was, he understood what she was going through, understood her suffering and her pain. Even though she had been brought up in a church, she had never experienced Jesus as caring about her. But there he was, a fellow sufferer. Somehow she found the courage to go on, now with a companion, wounded as she was wounded.

The Christian gospel is centered on a God who was not a remote King or Lord, but a fellow sufferer, who is with us in our pain, who stands with us in our tragedy and who takes upon himself the evil we experience. Reread Chapter Three about Jesus the Christ, and Chapter Six about salvation, and that will be the Savior you will encounter. While we will never explain, let alone explain away, the problem of suffering, we are not stuck with the dilemma posed at the beginning of this chapter. The premises are all wrong, and if you start out with the wrong premises there is no way to arrive at the right conclusion. If Jesus is Emmanuel, God with us, then God is our fellow sufferer. And that God is not outside our experience, but intimately related to it.

We do not expect to be magically relieved of evil and suffering. As William Sloane Coffin put it following the death of his son in an automobile accident, "In God there is minimum protection, but maximum support."

The struggle for many thoughtful Christians is maintaining that there is a creative life force at the root of everything—what we have called God—and simultaneously affirming that this force has a will and a purpose. Yet we must live in the tension of these two affirmations. What is more, the community of faith continually affirms that we stand in covenant relationship with this willful and gracious source of purpose.

The one recorded prayer of Jesus that was not affirmatively answered pleaded, "Father, let this cup pass from me." In Jesus we know that God is with us in whatever we face. It is not that faith saves us from tragedy, from evil and from the misadventures that afflict every one of us if we live long enough, but that God saves us right in the midst of our suffering. Remember that in the Hebrew myth, when Adam and Eve lost Eden, God lost it too. Since that time every victory we have won has been with God and every problem that has defeated us has broken God's heart. Even so, as we shall see in Chapter Eleven, the story is not yet over, and we live out the years of our lives, not with faith in ourselves nor with the confidence that everything for us will be all right, but holding the amazing affirmation that whatever we face, God is with us—closer than breathing and nearer than hands or feet.

8

The Church and the Reign of God

We now come to the matter of how the dynamic energy, the power with a purpose we call God, is evidenced both in individuals and in society. The Christian faith is not a theoretical enterprise. As Jesus was not an idea, an image, or a seeming presence, but rather flesh and blood, so God's activity in the Christian era takes on a visible shape and an institutional form, just as it had done throughout history to that time. In our era we call this social reality "the church."

Synagogue and Church in Christian Scriptures

The word *church*, translated from the Greek, literally means "the called out." Those who heard the gospel, and became committed as a result to live different lives and to reorder their social context, made up this new entity. The "church" found its initial expression in small neighborhood or home-based clusters of the faithful. Early on these groups of neighbors and friends existed in juxtaposition to similar groupings among the Jews called "synagogues." The Greek word from which *synagogue* comes is literally translated, "the gathered together."

As long as Christians were still considered to constitute a sect of Judaism, they met in synagogues—as was Jesus' custom during his ministry (Luke 4:16). When "Christian" synagogues became increasingly dominated by both a Gentile constituency and mindset, the term *church* became the more common designation.

The word *church* is foreign to the gospels and to the ministry of Jesus. It is used by Jesus on only two occasions. In responding to Peter's confession that he was the Messiah, Jesus said, "On this rock I will build my church…" (Matthew 16:18). Jesus also counsels his hearers that in handling disputes among Christians, certain matters should be taken to the church (Matthew 18:17). This paucity of evidence seems to suggest that these may not be authentic statements of Jesus, but were added later to clarify specific concerns that had arisen in the life of the community. Apart from these two texts, the word never appears in the Gospels. This is particularly startling when we recall that the Gospels were put together by the church decades after it was launched.

Luke, in his biographical sketch of Jesus, never employs the word, and it does not appear in his Acts of the Apostles until Chapter 5. The events of Pentecost are described in some detail, but even though we call that occasion the birthday of the church, the word is not mentioned.

Christian Scriptures, apart from Matthew, Mark, Hebrews, and some of the minor epistles, are predominantly the products of the world of the Gentiles. Yet even Paul, the primary author, uses the word *church* sparingly. In Romans, the document that outlines his basic theology, Paul employs it only three times, and then the references are limited to the final sixteenth chapter in which he sends greetings to friends. Clearly for Paul, when speaking theologically, the church was not a rigidly bound institutional reality, subject to an authoritative definition, but the way to talk about a social phenomenon.

Jesus, and the Reign of God

If, however, the activity of God working in and through a community of faith was to have visibility, the locus of that visibility had to be identified. Jesus talked at length about God's activity, but used another term to identify it. Jesus' emphasis was not on what his followers would do but on what God was already doing. When Jesus used the term "the *kingdom*—or *reign*—of God," he was not discussing a human organization. Neither he nor his followers would produce it. It was already taking shape as God was working powerfully and with purpose—back to our basic definition of God. Jesus saw his role as the one who came to announce its presence and call others to observe what it was about.

While traditionally we have referred to it as "the kingdom of God," that may be a mistranslation thrust on us by scholars working under the authority of another king, the king of England. To get away from thinking of God as a being—a king—we will use the designation "the reign of God," which may even be a more accurate translation from the Greek. Jesus was not describing a place, a kingdom, or a territory, but a condition, a way of life, a dynamic that increasingly was in evidence wherever God was seen to be at work.

John the Baptist came proclaiming, "The kingdom [reign] of heaven has come near" (Matthew 3:2)—that is, God's authority is about to take visible form. Matthew is the representative of the more orthodox Jews among the four evangelists, and Jews hesitated to employ the term *God* either verbally or in writing. But when we examine the Gospel parallels, it is clear that what he called, "the reign of heaven," or just "the Reign," Mark, Luke and the author of the Fourth Gospel called the "reign of God." God was at work within history establishing a new order. It was this notion that God's purpose was taking on a fresh expression, which constituted the centerpiece of Jesus' public teaching ministry.

Jesus' message from the beginning of his ministry was a reiteration of the Baptist's declaration. According to Mark, Jesus' first public proclamation was, "The kingdom of God has come near." (Mark 1:15) Here was creative energy at work.

The preponderance of Jesus' teachings either testified to or made visible the presence of this new reality. Many of the short sayings as well as the longer parables begin, "The kingdom of God is like…," and most of his mighty works were seen as demonstrations of its presence. While the disciples, and others with ears to hear, could observe it, it was God who was producing it—and it was on the way!

These days we talk about paradigm shifts, wholly different ways to think and to act. God's reign was to produce that sort of revolution! Its coming would disturb and reorder all the normal ways folks lived and society functioned.

Consider just a few of the references in Matthew's account, for example, and observe what God's reign looks like compared to the way things were in the world it was about to penetrate. In God's reign the poor in spirit and the persecuted are the possessors; it comes to a Roman soldier and is missed by many of Jesus' pious countrymen; forgiveness and turning the other cheek replace an eye for an eye; it is like an inconspicuous seed that would grow into a mighty tree, and a particle of yeast that would infiltrate and alter the entire lump of dough; children are the most honored; the rich have a very difficult time entering; the economics are different—the last are first and those who work one hour are paid the same as those who work all day; tax collectors and harlots are honored guests. Matthew's account is replete with references to the power and presence of this Reign. The word is employed fifty-four times.

In Luke, who also uses the term generously, everything commonly accepted as normal is turned upside down. The unrighteous are welcomed; women are not only respected but are often the heroes; the rotten son who could not wait until his father died so he could get his share of the inheritance, is honored with the party; Roman officials and tax collectors are called just and Pharisees are ridiculed; the Samaritan acts like a neighbor; the beggar is welcomed in Abraham's bosom, while the rich man roasts in Hades. Justice and equity replace obedience to a legal code, and those the pious didn't want around lead the parade.

The point is made over and over again: the rules that govern this new order are nothing like the rules set down by the jurisdictions that dominated the old order. Something new is on the way, and Jesus' mighty works evidence that the revolution was already taking form in the midst of society— Jewish and Roman.

The Fourth Gospel uses the term only twice, both times in a conversation between Jesus and Nicodemus, during which the ruler of the Jews is told that the only way to enter the reign of God is to be born again. God is at work remaking human hearts and reordering society. Nothing will be the same. Again, neither social engineering nor religious works will produce it. This reign is an activity and a gift of God.

The disciples' initial role, according to Jesus, was to pray for it—and we still do almost every time we gather. But beware! Could there be anything more frightening than to receive a positive answer to the petition, "thy kingdom come, thy will be done on earth as it is in heaven"? Few of us are at all certain we are prepared for the changes the full revelation of God's new ways to live would bring to our lives. We are all too comfortable with the old order, which has placed most of those who read this book in positions of some wealth and privilege. Yet this prayer rolls off our lips as if it meant nothing. By this petition we are asking that all of our systems, our governments, our economics and our values be transformed by God so that they reflect a radical, new, social reality.

When the new age did begin to take visible form in the ministry of Jesus, the righteous were horrified, as are the most pious in our own time. As evidences of the reign of God materialized, those with a passionate commitment to and a vested interest in the old order were scandalized, and the one who heralded its coming, Jesus of Nazareth, was put to death.

The Church and the Reign of God

After Jesus, the term *reign of God,* slowly fell into disuse, and was replaced by notions centering around a new image: the church. The question, therefore is: Do we mean by the term, *church* the same thing Jesus meant by *reign of God?* Or is the church, as a human institution, only a pale reflection of what God was about to bring? We must conclude that the church falls far short of Jesus' image of God's new order. And yet here and there, now and then, among this group and that we can detect evidences, outcroppings, intimations of what God has been at work to establish quite beyond our wisdom, skill, and commitment. The church is not the Reign, but at its best may bear the initial marks of the new order. The Christian life was occasionally referred to as "The Way." Christians were called to live lives that gave evidence of the reality of God's mighty works within history, but Christians did not replicate the Reign as they organized the church. God provided the way. Christians were called to walk it.

As theologians earlier in the twentieth century often put it, the reign of God—they called it the Kingdom—is already in our midst, but it is always still on the way.

If there is a relationship, however partial, between the reign of God and the church, it is in how clearly the latter reflects the former. As did Jesus in his ministry, the task of the called out is to offer evidence that God's reign is on the way, in fact is here, albeit only partially. While we pray that it might fully come on earth as it is in heaven, obviously that is not now the case. The church, however, is the forward party, God's expeditionary force, which carves out a beachhead in territory occupied by the old order. Or we might think of the church as God's demonstration project. Its task is to provide a foretaste of how things will be when the "kingdom of the world has become the kingdom of our Lord and of his Messiah, and he will reign for ever and ever" (Revelation 11:15b).

The church, therefore, seeks to discover the will of God, through the great conversation (see Chapter Five), calls its adherents to live according to that design, and demonstrates the reality of what is not yet fully present.

The Functions of the Church

Consider the basic functions, which take place in most congregations, in light of the above definition of the church's essential nature.

- The worship of the church centers around a feast of praise and thanksgiving—a eucharist, to use the Greek word for thanksgiving—and a proclamation that the fullness of God's reign is at hand. In worship the work of Christ is remembered, the community celebrates its life, and the final victory of God is affirmed.

- The evangelistic task of the church is the proclamation of the good news of the coming reign of God and the calling of others to share in the demonstration of its presence. Evangelism has little to do with finding unchurched people, meeting their personal needs, creating for them a friendly and comfortable environment, and making them members of a social group. Nor is it the evangelistic task to purify them so that God will love them enough to take them to heaven. (See Chapter Six.)

- The mission of the church is both to proclaim with power the activity of God in establishing a new order, and to give that order visibility. The church says by what it is and what is does: "Do you want to see how things will be when God finally brings the Reign to full fruition? We will show you." The message was first of all for the Jews, but ultimately for the whole world.

- The service performed by the church is its embodying of a lifestyle inherent in the new order God is bringing to birth. If in the old order the world's people are divided by race, class, gender, politics, and condition, in the new order all of these distinctions disappear. Persons are accepted and loved not because they are righteous but because they exist. God is at work breaking down every barrier and creating one new humanity. The first barrier to go was between Jew and Gentile, but in that reconciliation were the seeds of universal justice, goodwill and mutual acceptance.

• The educational task of the church derives from the proclamation and embodying of all the law and the prophets—namely, a love for God and a love for others. In its ministries of teaching and learning the church reflects on its faith.

• The goal toward which the entire enterprise moves is a recapitulation of God's work in Christ, who came to reconcile the world to Godself. Those in Christ were new creations, part of a whole revolutionary way to live. The old was passing away and the new was on the way. Christ, the reconciler (see Chapter Three), had now put in the hands of what became known as the church, "the ministry of reconciliation" (2 Corinthians 5:16–21).

The church, therefore, is that body of people who reach into God's future, bring back a piece of it and put it on display in the here and now. Even as it performs this task it does so fully cognizant of its own imperfection, and aware of the terrible compromises it makes with the old order. Yet the church acts on behalf of God despite its fragmentation and the failures of the sinful people who populate, serve, and lead it. We live in the community of faith as if we were already living in the new order.

With all its limitations, the church at its best is a very different social reality. It has been caught up by God in the new age. Its people have been breathed upon by the Holy Spirit (Chapter Four) and made alive, reborn in Christ. Through baptism they have shared in Christ's death and raised in his likeness. And when the old order acts as if it were still in total control, the church announces its defeat and declares that as the new age dawns the old authorities have been disarmed. This bold affirmation is not made on the basis of the church's own strength, but on the basis of God's powerful and purposeful activity. The church, therefore, no longer needs to cooperate with the principalities and powers as if they were still in command. We live and work as if God's reign were already fully present.

Marks of the Faithful Church

To change the image: If Christ is all of God we can see and experience in human form, and if the church, as Paul defined it, is the body of Christ, then the church has been called out to be all of God the world can see in our time and place. As did Jesus, we both herald it and demonstrate what it is about. Everything else churchly must be understood in terms of its relationship to the reign of God—present and on the way. The implications are enormous. Consider just a few of them.

- Since God is one and the reign of God the product of this one God, the church is one church. The divisions that have arisen in it are testimonies to its sinfulness and must be confessed as such. While there obviously exist multiplicities of congregations in any community, and hundreds of different ecclesial bodies worldwide, there is but the one church, since there is but the one reign of God.

- Being a reflection of God's coming reign, the church does not belong to its members, to its denominational officials, or to anyone else. The church belongs to God through Jesus the Christ. "With his own blood he bought her and for her life he died."

- Nevertheless, the church will speak the language of the people around it, and that language will differ from place to place. Even though the church is one church, since the reign of God is one reign, it will take on differing shapes and manifestations depending on its geographic, philosophic, and social contexts. It may also look very different in one era than it does in another. The church in the United States at the beginning of the twenty-first Christian century will not look like, sound like, or act like the European church of the twelfth century—East or West. This means that any attempt to freeze its life at any particular time and place, and make that specimen a model for every time and every place, is a violation of its nature. Not even what is referred to as the New Testament church is a for-all-times model. Even in its formative period the church was markedly different in one place than it was in another. Yet it was one church—at least by design.

- God is not limited to the church. The church may reflect God's presence and God's activity, but it does not exhaust it. God may not even be limited to Christians or to anything about our religious practices, doctrines, and perspectives. To assume that the church has any sort of significance upon which God is dependent, has moved it beyond its assigned borders into the fields of idolatry.

- The church thus defined is not eternal. While it seems to be the way God is working with us now, this power with a purpose is not static, and is not stuck with any institution or combination of institutions. "The wind blows where it will." The time may come when the church will disappear. That occurrence will not spell the end of God, just the end of a way we understand God to be at work. Even so, for now the church is that community of faith and witness breathed upon by the Holy Spirit and sharing in God's redemptive work. Its nature is to proclaim and demonstrate the reality of the coming reign of God.

2

The Christian Life

Theology is fundamentally about God, not about us. The theological discipline may deal with and discuss how we understand God, but it is not centered on our response. That response is properly called "religion." You will note that the substantial chapters of this book thus far have dealt with: God, Jesus the Christ, the Holy Spirit, the Bible, the cross, the problem of evil, and the reign of God. At every point we have focused on God's activity and how we understand it. At best, theological inquiry can examine the Christian life only as derivative of our understanding of God.

Liberals traditionally ask the question, "What are we Christians about as we seek to be faithful to God?" In this book we have been asking quite another question: "What is God about, and how can we understand, receive, and celebrate God's activity?"

Even though the preceding chapter discussed the church as a human institution, our focus was really on the new order of things Jesus heralded and God had established. We call that new order "the reign of God." In this chapter we will discuss the Christian life. But as the church is derivative of the reign of

God, so the Christian life is our individual response to the activity of God.

God's Grace, and Our Response

Again we encounter a word that may be at the core of our faith. It is *grace*. Historically, the word has been defined as the unmerited favor and love of God. By grace we mean that God's love is not conditioned or dependent on anything we do. It is a gift. The concept of grace holds powerful implications even if we are limited to a notion of God that sees him as a being or a person who presides over the world from a distance.

Grace takes on even greater significance if our understanding of God is the energy, the power with a purpose, that not only gives everything meaning, but is the meaning of everything. God not only creates the process that gives the world its shape and dynamic, God is that shape and dynamic. Thus it all depends on God. And when everything depends on God, and God is loving—or love in action—then grace must stand at the heart of authentic religion. It is not that "man proposes and God disposes," but that God not only proposes, but also sets the context for the human agenda, and thus all human response.

This response to God's activity is called *religion*. In our tradition we may even more narrowly call it "the Christian life." Everything about our faith flows from what God has already graciously done. Christian theology affirms a perspective that may not be unique among the religions of the world, but is certainly not commonly held. If in most religions, obedience to God's laws—right belief and right action—serve the purpose of appeasing the deity, Christians affirm that there is nothing we can do to earn God's favor. It is a gift. God does not act, graciously or punitively, in response to our righteousness or lack of it. God acts first, loves first, gives first, and seeing that love, which we do not deserve and have not earned, we respond with thanksgiving.

Salvation is all grace.

Good works, all gratitude.

We do not offer sacrifices so that God will look favorably upon us. We do not worship and pray so that God will pay attention to the drought and make it rain. We do not offer our children so that God will understand how much we fear him, and bless us—or at least refrain from doing us in. Whatever works we perform are offerings of thankful hearts. God's grace is expressed in a loving goodwill that is built into the universe prior to our doing anything! God's creative goodness is inherent in the world whether we see it, acknowledge it, or follow it. The Christian life is the way we thankfully move with and under the power flow that is always at work. We know about this love most clearly as we discover it in the life and ministry of Jesus the Christ.

How the Reformation Saw It

As Karl Barth suggested, "Jesus loves me" may still be the most profound Christian sentiment anyone can express. While theologians throughout history have affirmed the centrality of God's love and grace, leaders of the Reformation went to great pains to spell it out. John Calvin was so profoundly convinced that everything depended on God, he held that even the response we make is a gift God gives. God may only give it to a few, "the elect," but Calvin held that the rest have no right to complain because the fact that anyone is forgiven shows how gracious God is. Martin Luther left a bit more room for free will, but free-wheeling free will, even to him, seemed to deny the authority of God.

Reformation theologians were fighting off a religious institution that held itself up as having the authority to decide who should or should not enter the path to salvation in this life and the gate to heaven in the next. They were equally distressed that the Christian faith had degenerated into a way individuals could win God's favor by performing good works or believing right doctrine. God, they held, not any human institution, was the author of history and the arbiter of salvation.

The debate over how far free will went raged for a long time, and perhaps still does. Long before the Reformation, Christian theologians were clear about the primacy of God's action and the futility of works as the key to God's mercy. Paul, in Romans, his basic theological testimony, makes it abundantly clear that no one is made righteous by works of the law. While Paul was referring specifically to the law of Moses, throughout the book of Romans he asserts that it is God's grace alone that counts, not any righteous work we perform or obedience to any sort of law—except the law of love, and even that is a thankful response to what God has already done.

Today's Popular Religion

Nevertheless, despite all the historic testimony that comes to us in the great conversation, many contemporary Protestants assume that if we live moral lives, believe the right doctrines, and don't violate the Ten Commandments, God may decide to love us. At the most mundane level, how many bad jokes have you heard about Peter at the pearly gates deciding who should enter and who should not, based on what they had done? The grievous problem is that significant numbers of church women and men believe, or seem to believe, that these jokes describe how it really works!

Many Christians are also puzzled by the doctrine of original sin. It is difficult to understand how Adam and Eve did us all in. It may help to realize that the story of the Garden of Eden is just that, a story, a mythological attempt to answer basic questions that plagued human consciousness from the beginning: Why is there suffering? Why do we die? Why does the earth seem so unfriendly? Why is there hostility among people? Was there a time when everything was perfect— and will there ever be such an epoch again? These stories were developed over long periods of time as ways to think about and deal with basic philosophic and religious questions. We take stories seriously, but *they are stories!*

As we saw in Chapter Seven, the old saying "In Adam's fall we sinned all" is an unsatisfactory answer to the problem of suffering. But this much is clear: we are separated from God and from what we ought to and yearn to be. And that condition is called "sin." The fact that it infects the whole system and everyone in it—and always has—is really what is meant by original sin.

Despite the mythological attempt to answer the question in Genesis, it is abundantly clear that something is amiss in the world. It is also abundantly clear that we humans have never solved the problem of sin and never will. We cannot get back to God on our own. Healing the multiple rifts is up to God, and our faith tells us that God has acted, is acting, and will act to reconcile us to Godself. The Christian life is only our joyful response to that activity.

Justification

For Christians, the heart of God's reconciling act is seen in Jesus the Christ. If we are to be made right, it is not by our effort but by God's love. This power with a purpose has been at work all along, "reconciling the world to Godself." The word that is part of the traditional theological vocabulary is *justification*. It comes initially from Paul's letter to the Romans where he holds that we are justified—that is made right—not by works, but in thankful response to God's gift.

Paul calls this response, "faith." Faith is not belief in right doctrine, or even an effort at right conduct. It is thankful trust in the God who has been at work, is at work, and will be at work to reconcile all things to Godself.

For Christians this act of God is the good news, the gospel. God has not wandered off on other pursuits, nor is God a dispassionate judge who sits in the sky like a heavenly highway patrol officer looking for speeders—or sinners. God is the very substance of life that is with us and in us, as God is with and in all things. And thus it is the reconciliation of all things that becomes the goal of history. In Romans 8:19ff, Paul talks about the whole creation waiting to be reconciled, along with humanity. It is a cosmic, not just a personal, end point of joy and victory toward which everything is moving with God. More about that in our final chapter.

Grace and Good Works

Seeing what God has done, accepting the good news, we participate with God in the salvation of the world. We take on, by God's commission, the proclamation of the message of reconciliation. The bearing of this witness in word and deed constitutes the Christian life. Everything else is subsidiary.

We don't worship, serve, study, pray, and evangelize in order to be Christians. We do these things because we already are. They do not make us acceptable. God has already declared our acceptance in Jesus the Christ, and all of these activities of faith constitute our grateful response.

Christians bear the fruit of the Spirit, not in order to be righteous, but because God has accepted us. A tree does not produce apples in order to become an apple tree, but because it already is. The love, joy, peace, patience, kindness, goodness, gentleness, faithfulness, and self-control that constitute the fruit of the Christian life (Galatians 5:22) come upon us and work within us because God has already declared us to be justified. The Christian is set free to live and work with God as part of the redemptive process to which all creation must be the eventual heir. Yet none of this depends on us. It all depends on God.

When I was a young person, one of my favorite religious poems held that:

> God has no hands but our hands to do his work today.
> He has no feet but our feet to lead men in the way.

As I grew older I came to realize that God may use my hands and my feet, but God is not dependent on me. I am dependent on God. By God's grace I was born in a Christian home in a Christian culture, nurtured in a faithful Christian church. I chose none of these things. They came as gifts. To think of my faith as something I developed independently is arrogant and faithless. Even so, I am not essential to God's mission. God can get along without me, and shortly shall!

Since it is all a matter of grace and not of works, Christians never legitimately ask the question addressed by the lawyer to whom Jesus told the story of the good Samaritan. You may remember the inquiry: "What must I do to inherit eternal life?" (Luke 10:25b). His question was a request for the minimum qualifications, as if one had to put so many good works in the slot before it would deliver God's gift. "What is the minimum amount of work I have to do to pass this class?" Perhaps the most difficult thing for modern men and women to hear is that there are no minimum qualifications. God has taken the initiative, and even our affirmative response is a gift we have been offered.

Cheap Grace

Many theologians in the past, including Dietrich Bonhoeffer, have warned us about cheap grace. God's gifts are free, but they are not cheap. An extraordinary amount of discipline is involved in the Christian life. Our task is enormous; to proclaim the gift of God through Jesus the Christ, and to work for the reconciliation of all things. But the key is that we take on this discipline and give ourself to this project, not to earn God's favor, but as the joyful response we call faith.

Those who follow the careers of athletes know that if they are to excel they must possess certain genetic gifts. But genes alone do not make a champion. It takes hours a day of training, practice, taking the body beyond where it has ever been before. No pain, no gain!

An athlete without discipline will not win. A Christian without the disciplines of the spirit will not be an adequate agent of reconciliation. No church is built, no victory for justice achieved, no evil system beaten back, no suffering relieved, no prejudice overcome, no peace secured without the blood of Christians flowing from wounds inflicted by those who will resist the will and the plan of God that the world be reconciled. To follow Jesus is to offer up one's life. To the extent our churches are populated with undisciplined Christians, the world is not being made whole. God may love spiritually flabby Christians, but they are useless as agents of reconciliation. Worship within the community of faith, reinforced by a disciplined life of prayer and praise, makes spiritually sturdy Christians.

Part of the discipline involves occasionally acting against what appears to be one's self-interest. Feeding the hungry may mean that I will not have as much food. More likely, standing by the persecuted may mean I will be persecuted. The history of faith is replete with stories of people of God who have spent much of their lives in jail. If you read the record of martyrs for the faith, you will discover a sturdy collection of men and women who were responding to God's love, not trying to earn it, and whose lives were freely given in that effort.

The Saints

As there is no such thing as faith apart from the God who gives it, there is no such thing as a solitary Christian. The word *saint* never appears in the Christian Scriptures. But the word *saints* appears sixty times! Faith is a community event. It is said that Jesus made disciples twelve at a time. The only spiritual athletes are team members. In the Hebrew Scriptures God's saving purpose was addressed to Israel, not to specific Israelites. Many contemporary religionists see faith as focusing on personal salvation. But in the Christian Scriptures it is not my salvation that is at the heart of things, but our salvation. It is the world God loved so much a son was sent. Obviously since we are part of that world, a very important part, we are included. Nevertheless, the Christian faith must always employ plural pronouns.

God was in Christ reconciling the world—that's all of us and then some. The central sacred act of the church, the Eucharist, is most commonly called "communion." It is the community that remembers Jesus and looks forward to the great banquet of heaven. The church's feast of thanksgiving is no time for people to sit alone meditating upon Jesus, any more than the family dinner is the time for members of the household to sit quietly by themselves with their solitary meals. The energy, the processes of life, that we call God, are societal processes. The Christian life, therefore, is lived out in the community of faith.

10

"New" Theologies—
Liberation, Feminist,
Ethnic

The Christian world these days seems awash with new
theologies. In recent times we have observed, among them,
these three: liberation theology, feminist theology, and ethnic
theology. The last two have sprung from the first, so even though
we will consider each one in turn, we will give major attention
to liberation theology.

Are There New Theologies?

Before we move to an analysis of these three ways to think
about God, we need to inquire as to how there can be any such
thing as a "new" theology. Isn't theology unaffected by current
events? Are not these religious nuisances just another indication
that the theological world is wandering about without any roots
or notions a person can count on year after year? If God is the
same yesterday, today, and forever, why can't we just accept the
Bible as God's word and believe that what it says will stand
forever? As musical styles float in and out of popularity, disap-
pearing with each setting sun, do we have to live in a world of
theological fads? Don't worry about rap, we're told. Five years

from now nobody will know what it is. Can the same be said of
these new theologies?

In an age when everything about religion seems to be coming unglued, these questions resonate positively with many lay
people. They are not interested in a new theology. They would
just like to get a better grip on what the Bible says.

Of course, those who harbor these misgivings are at least
partly correct in their assumptions. There are no new theologies! But there are new ways to look at theology. The essential
nature of God doesn't change from one age to the next. But
culture does, our experience of what is real does, and the perspective from which we see and understand both the world and
God's activity does. Since theology is a reflection on God from
a specific place and culture, and since culture is a dynamic, ever-
changing reality, theology is never static.

Reading the Bible in Context

Back in Chapter Two, about God, we suggested that the
ancient creeds of the church grew out of a way the people who
formed them understood their world. The creeds were products
of a particular philosophic system, or at least made sense only
in the context of that worldview. If for many modern Christians the great ecumenical creeds no longer provide the clearest
ways to understand God's relationship to us, it is not that God
has significantly changed, but that the way we understand the
world no longer derives from the philosophy common in the
fourth, fifth, and sixth Christian centuries.

We have long known that the serious Bible student cannot
take a Scriptural passage at random and understand what it
means without considering the context in which it is set. By
context we not only mean the verses or chapters surrounding
the particular text, but the world surrounding the author. Who
wrote it? To whom? Why? What problem was he addressing?
What in the culture shaped that problem? What was his point
of view? There is a world of difference in the issues confronting
the authors of the books of Revelation and the Song of Solomon.

We read each writer with some understanding of the context surrounding the generation of the particular text. The alternative is to view the Bible as a collection of magic verses, any one of which can be pulled out and used to make a point at any time about anything.

What is true of the Bible is true of our everyday experiences. How we view any given circumstance is conditioned by what else is going on in our immediate vicinity and in our own time. If in the early history of the Hebrews, God was conceived to be a tribal deity, and only later as the one God of all, and finally, in Jesus, as a God of love, we do not infer by this transition that God grew up.

Jesus told his followers that even if the ancient texts talked about justice in terms of an eye for an eye, there was now a new ethic in which people turned the other cheek and gave good when they had received evil. It is doubtful that even the most rigorous biblical fundamentalists would see that ethical alteration as a sign that God had matured or changed his mind. We make sense of the biblical witness only when we know that the context of the tribes of Jahweh, which invaded Canaan under Joshua, was radically different than that which surrounded the author of the Sermon on the Mount.

In Chapter Five, in which we discussed the authority of the Bible, the point was made that every text must be understood in terms of the worldview, background, philosophy, history, and daily experiences of those who first told and then later wrote and collected the stories. There are in the Scriptures scores of seeming contradictions. Is it that one writer was wrong and another correct? Or can we not assume that each one wrote out of a particular context?

When, for instance, the writer of Psalm 137 talks about the joy one would get from taking the infants of the Babylonians and smashing their skulls against the rocks, is it assumed that infanticide is divinely sanctioned? The psalm is the bitter lament of a poet in captivity, stripped of a homeland and devastated by the loss of everything important.

To take any text and understand it without considering the historic context of those who produced it is the recipe for a distorted approach to Bible study. If you want the big word for this awareness, it is *contextualization.*

Likewise, for any contemporary Christian, the Bible doesn't change with our circumstances, and God doesn't wear different sets of clothes for different occasions. But how we understand both Scripture and God is profoundly conditioned by what else is going on in our lives at the time we consider any text or the theology behind it. We must not only come to terms with the context of the writer, but with the context of the reader!

In addition to understanding the Bible contextually, consider how we must look differently at this problem if our notion of God is dynamic, not static. If God is not only involved in the process of life but is also the life force that is always breaking out in new ways; if God is power with a purpose, always reaching creatively into the future, then as the world is forever in a state of flux—moving in a clear direction—so may be God.

If we are on a journey of faith, and if the future is unknown because it has yet to happen, and if God is the source of energy that generates everything that takes place, then as we encounter new experiences, so does God. If the universe is expanding in every direction all the time at the speed of light, then God is not through creating. God, being intimately related to the creation, is therefore living in a dynamic relationship to both the creative process and to creation itself.

We now are prepared to look at these three "new" theologies with two propositions in mind: (1) How we understand God and thus all of theology is conditioned by our own perspectives and immediate circumstances; (2) God is dynamic, in motion, struggling, generating, involved with the creation.

Liberation Theology

We begin our sketch of liberation theology by looking at the context out of which it came: namely, Latin American Catholicism, and the dynamic events taking place on that conti-

nent in the wake of Vatican II. But it is not simply the big international movements and events that set the stage for liberation
theology, but the conditions and aspirations of the poor in Latin
America.

A few pastors and theologians were able to articulate how a
new dynamic within Catholicism and the cries of the poor in-
tersected in fresh and exciting ways. These theologians were not
remote from the problems of their people, but knew and shared
the pain of the oppressed. As they were repeatedly encountered
by the God of the gospel, they grew uncomfortable with the
religious approach common on their continent.

Throughout Latin America everything rested on and was
controlled by a three-legged political stool:

Leg 1—the wealthy oligarchy and landed aristocracy
Leg 2—the military, which controlled most governments
Leg 3—the Catholic church

As a result, practically all the wealth and power resided in
the hands of very few people. Most folk lived as slaves to this
trinity of powers. The oligarchy owned everything. The military provided the security. The church controlled the common
people and gave the other two legs of the stool their moral authority.

As long as all of the bishops and most of the priests were
sent to Latin America from Spain and Portugal, and were content to enjoy the privileges they automatically received by being
part of the power structure, chances of radical change were remote. Following Vatican II, the first indigenous bishops were
appointed. Up until then Latin America had never had a single
bishop born in that continent!

With the appointment of "native" bishops and pastors, it
became popular in many Catholic parishes to teach the common people simple reading so they could study the Bible. It was
in the context of Bible study that first the pastors and bishops,
and then lay Christians, became aware that their problems had
been faced before, and that the Bible held a record of those

encounters. That is, they began to read the Bible contextually, and to identify their own context with particular biblical episodes and the context of those ancient people of God.

No group of stories had more effect on them than the sagas that surrounded the Exodus. Here were people with whom they could relate, whose problems were much the same as their own. They were poor, oppressed, held captive. Their condition had not changed for hundreds of years. Their situation seemed hopeless. But God had a purpose for them, and had determined they should be set free. Moses was sent to them, and in what appeared to be a revolution, during which the firstborn in every Egyptian household was killed, they finally escaped Pharaoh's bondage.

The poor of Latin America noted that God had not only willed the liberation of the Hebrews, but had acted as the liberator. Moses was God's spokesperson, but the energy, the dynamic, and the liberating power rested in God's hands. They also realized that throughout history God's purpose has been to set free those who were in captivity. That is what you see when you read the Bible through the eyes of the captives!

When Jesus began his ministry at his home synagogue in Nazareth, he announced that the liberation of the oppressed was to be at the center of his work. And he quoted Isaiah, another spokesperson for God, the liberator.

> He (God) has anointed me to bring good news to the poor. He has sent me to proclaim release to the captives and recovery of sight to the blind, to let the oppressed go free, to proclaim the year of the Lord's favor.
>
> (Luke 4:18–19)

The more they looked at both the Bible and the record of God's work in the world, the more these oppressed Latin Americans became convinced that liberation was the heart of theology. Everything began to be viewed from that perspective. God was in the business of setting captives free!

What is more, the Scriptures made it clear that God was not in a neutral corner in the fight for freedom. While God might have been the God of all, God took a position, and so did Jesus, and so did the prophets. God sided with the oppressed. Or as it was subsequently put, "God has a preferential option for the poor."

This idea about God, this theology, has obvious religious implications. Remember that religion is how we respond to God. God did not live in heaven or in the great ornate cathedrals. God lived right in the midst of the people, and as they suffered God suffered too. The story of Jesus' death and the hope of his resurrection became their central story. Religion, they decided, should be exercised as close to God as possible, right in the neighborhoods of the poor. Since most of these people were villagers, unused to the complex ways of the city, they organized small house churches in their neighborhoods, where the Bible could be studied and the "project" of liberation planned and executed.

While liberation theology grew out of the experiences and hopes of the poor, pastors and theologians were able to articulate it verbally and in writing.

Dom Helder Camara was the bishop of the poorest part of northeastern Brazil. While he had always done what he could to care for the needs of the poor, their liberation became a powerful component of his ministry. Since he had originally come from the ruling class, not everybody among his old friends and colleagues applauded his new interest in social justice. It is reported that he once said, "When I feed the hungry, they call me a saint. When I ask why they are hungry, they call me a Communist." He continued to ask, in increasingly embarrassing ways, why the prevailing social and economic structure doomed so many of his people to hunger and poverty. On another occasion he said, "I can spend all day pulling people out of the river, but sooner or later I must go up the river to see who is throwing them in."

There were other academics and members of various Catholic orders, who not only worked with the poor but whose scholarly hunger led them to do research, write, and teach. Among them was a Peruvian priest named Gustavo Gutierrez, who authored the book that became the linchpin for liberation thought: *A Theology of Liberation.*

What is the theological substance that undergirds liberation theology? Is it a new theology, a new way to understand God? Quite the contrary. It is strikingly biblical, flows from what we have always known about God, and is well within the orthodox tradition of the church. Jesus Christ came to set the captives free. That is the heart of all liberation thought. Its uniqueness lies in the context out of which it sprung. Liberation theology, in its simplest terms, is looking at the gospel through the eyes of the poor. It is how the oppressed see the work of Christ in history and in their midst.

Several years ago I authored a book, now out of print, entitled *A Guide to Liberation Theology for Middle-Class Congregations.* I sent a copy of it to Gustavo Gutierrez. When I subsequently saw him at a conference, he was gracious in his appreciation of my effort, but commented that, of course, it was very difficult to see the gospel through the eyes of the poor if you are not poor. That is to say, while we of the First World, who decide *what* we will eat and not *if* we will eat—the chief mark of affluence—can stand alongside and allow liberation theology to influence our understanding of the gospel, only the poor can be liberation theologians. Poverty is not the driving experience of my life. Certainly liberation theologians, Catholic and Protestant, have had a dramatic impact on the religious world, but the unpoor and the unhungry will never understand why "the poor heard him gladly," or what they found so appealing in Jesus' message.

If we have trouble hearing the gospel as the poor hear it, how much more difficult must it have been for the members of the Latin American oligarchy, the military, and the established church to hear it. They heard it as a Marxist plot. Even the pope viewed it with some suspicion, and censored several of the prominent theologians and pastors, who tried to flesh out the meaning of God's preferential option for the poor.

A similar situation prevailed in this country during the civil rights struggles a few decades ago. Decent ordinary churchmen and women in Northern as well as Southern churches saw civil rights as an anti-Christian, subversive, communist design. It should be no secret that freedom for the oppressed never comes as good news to the oppressors, who will do anything they can to fight it off.

The well-placed in Jesus' day viewed what he said and did with suspicion, while the poor understood that the reign of God meant their liberation. It was not impossible for the well-to-do to enter that reign, he held, just difficult; as difficult as it was to get a camel through a needle's eye. For us in the United States, among the affluent of the world, who consume 40 percent of the world's resources while we are only 6 percent of the population, it is also difficult to hear and understand what the poor have discovered in the gospel. Difficult, not impossible! It is as we sit quietly at the feet of the poor and learn from them that we are given ears to hear.

Liberation theology has provided the poor, not only in Latin America but throughout the world, a new voice. By the grace of God we have been given the privilege of hearing them proclaim, just as was done on the day of Pentecost, "God's deeds of power" (Acts 2:11b).

Feminist Theology

Feminist theology, again, is not really a new theology, but a way to look at the faith through the eyes of women. This issue is complicated by the fact that the great preponderance of theologians, authors, interpreters, and ecclesiastical officials have been men. Not only were they men, but they lived and worked—therefore, saw the world—in terms of a patriarchal culture. It is difficult to go back into the biblical narrative or church history and find significant examples of those who viewed the world through the eyes of women. While the Bible is replete with feminine heroes, Miriam, Hannah, Ruth, Mary, and many more, they lived in a culture that made certain patriarchal assumptions.

Feminist theologians have pointed out that in many places the biblical narrative is brutal and demeaning to women. In the story of Sodom (Genesis 18:9ff), when the city's ruffians demand that Lot send out to them his two male visitors, Lot, who did not want to be a bad host, counters by offering his two virgin daughters!

Elsewhere in the scriptural record women are dealt with more humanely. The Gospel of Luke is graced with many stories about women. Scholars have suggested that if a woman was not the original author, Luke got most of his materials from women, and handled what he found appreciativly.

Paul can be read both ways. On one hand he insists that women be subservient to their husbands and silent in church. On the other hand he declares that in Christ all distinctions, including those between the sexes, have disappeared. It has been suggested that when he is speaking of a social phenomenon and pleading that good order be maintained in the church and in family life he tends to reflect the sexism of his day. But when he is speaking theologically he is much more open to a nonsexist perspective. Nevertheless, many women have felt excluded and marginalized by Pauline texts.

Throughout church history it has been widely assumed that God is a male. Practically all the biblical language supports that assumption. The fact that all the writers, as far as we know, were men should make that reality come as no surprise. While there are occasional feminine allusions, the preponderance of the language is masculine. "Father, Son, and Holy Spirit" is a gender-specific allusion. In addition, God is almost always referred to using a masculine pronoun, "he." Feminine theologians have lifted up feminine images of God and have called women to take their rightful, powerful place in the new order of things God will and is bringing. We have called that new order "the reign of God."

Increasingly theologians, feminist and otherwise, have concluded that the root of the difficulty is seeing God as a person or a being with all the limitations that entails. Since all persons we know anything about are referred to as "he" or "she," to think of God in other ways than as a being opens up fresh possibilities. When God is not limited to human-like characteristics, such as gender, we can do theology without the burden of sexist distinctions and difficulties. "Heavenly father" always comes out "he." "Power with a purpose," or "the energy at the heart of everything," has no gender.

While it may round out our notion of God to think of "her" as well as "he," that approach still casts God as a being, who has a specific sexual identity. Obviously the use of both masculine and feminine metaphors is better than being limited to a male deity, but moving beyond seeing God as gender-specific may be better yet.

In this book we are concerned with how the context out of which we operate conditions how we define and relate to God. To see God through the eyes of feminist theologians frees us from other more limited perspectives. If our male God is too small, feminists have helped us enlarge that vision.

For other feminists the problem is not so much one of sexism as it is hierarchy. Any model that places anyone in a superior or an inferior position is called into question.

It is from feminists we have become more aware that the designation of God as King or Lord or in some cases even Father, flows from an imperialistic cultural model. Feminist theologians have been helpful, therefore, in developing language that is not only inclusive but cognizant that royal and feudal models for God are insufficient and inaccurate.

Black Theology

Ethnic theologies of all sorts arise from the particularities inherent in any given culture. Since each context is different, it should come as no surprise that ways in which diverse peoples experience God, and the metaphors used to define that experience, will differ. Since this book will be more readily used by a North American audience, by way of illustration we will look briefly at the most compelling of the ethnic theologies recently developed in this part of the world. We refer to black theology.

There has been, since the days when the first slaves were brought to this continent and evangelized, a particular reading of theological concerns within the black Christian community. Under slavery, and in the decades following emancipation, it took two distinct avenues. On one hand there was the theme of freedom. The sweet chariot that was to swing low and carry the slaves home, did not have heaven as its destination, but the North.

On the other hand, black religion tended to flow from a conservative, literalistic reading of the Bible, the sort that the white church not only approved, but also fostered. No one called it "black theology." The "colored" church tended to be evangelical and heavily controlled by black clergy. These community leaders, who managed to have in place their own personal power base, often depended for their position on the tacit support of leaders in the white society.

The coming of the civil rights movement effected a dramatic change in vital sectors of the black church. What we now call black theology or black liberation theology arrived with considerable energy in the 1960s. Its leaders were simultaneously activists in the civil rights movement and religious spokespersons. Demands were made on white churches for reparations. Pastors and other dedicated leaders saw white religion as a monolithic enemy. The most articulate spokesman was James Cone, a professor at Union Theological Seminary in New York.

While both feminist theology and black theology were indebted to the Latin American liberation theology, Cone and others tended to see their effort much more closely identified with a variety of liberation movements across the globe— principally among African Christians. As is the case with the two "new" theologies we have reviewed, black theology is a reading of faith through the eyes of an oppressed minority. And, as with the others, it often has a strident quality one expects and applauds anytime the oppressed find in God the hope for liberation.

Cone held that all Christian theology must be liberation theology, and any other sort was heretical. Cone went so far as to say that it is only as white people begin to hate their whiteness and long to be black that they can understand God. The only way for Pharaoh to understand the God of the Hebrews would have been for him to renounce his position and his Egyptianness and become a Hebrew. God, for Cone, was deeply concerned, perhaps exclusively concerned, with the oppressed. As with Gutierrez and his colleagues, black theologians looked at the whole Christian tradition through the eyes of the marginalized.

Our Context and the Great Conversation

In considering these new theologies we must ask a final question. How does the context in which our lives are cast inform our theology? Not every context is salutary. The white church in the pre-civil rights South lived in a culture that reinforced its role as oppressor, or at least put it in bed with the oppressors. If the local culture is the only voice one hears, then the theological result is bound to be as sinful as the societal context that conditions it. All new theologies, therefore, including the particular spin we put on the gospel, must be subject to the great conversation. Without hearing those voices and testing every point of view against them, the quest for God is bound to become distorted, if not demonic.

Each of us must ask how the particular world in which we live shapes or modifies our faith, but only in terms of that wider conversation. Whether or not we ask that question, we can be assured that we are profoundly affected by the philosophy, cultural values, worldview, politics, and social circumstances in which our lives are cast. Not to be aware of this dynamic is to assume that what we believe is carved out and handed down from heaven's eternal deposit of truth. We are profoundly influenced by our own particular culture. That is why in theology the great conversation is not a once-for-all exercise, but is a continuing testing of what we believe and what we are called as Christians to do.

11

God's Final Victory

In the spring of 1994 the most advanced telescope ever devised, hovering far above the earth as a satellite, observed in the farthest reaches of space an amazing phenomenon. While "black holes" had been thought theoretically possible for a number of years, the Hubble actually "saw" one. It was an estimated fifty million light years away, spinning at a million miles a second. So great was its gravitational force, it must have been the ultimate depository for millions of used-up stars. No light within hundreds of billions of miles will ever escape its appetite. If it were near enough, it would eat our Milky Way for lunch.

Granted enough time—a few trillion years, give or take a billion—is that how the universe and its history will end? If it all began with a big bang, will the last events take place as the universe slows down and finally stops, leaving the nothingness that was at the beginning—what Genesis calls the dark void?

The Consummation of History—The Power of Love

Theology takes seriously every scientific discovery, but looks at the consummation of history from a different perspective.

110 *Building a Biblical Faith*

While theologians affirm that God has been at the task of creation for a long time, and obviously has much yet to accomplish, we affirm that this creative energy is purposeful—power with a purpose. Creation is headed somewhere; and as God had the first word, so God will have the last. Nevertheless, God is not some external being who stands apart and dispassionately observes what is happening, giving directions to the natural order as a symphony conductor waves a baton at the players. God is the music, the wind and the friction between bow and string that creates the sound!

As throughout this book, we have talked about the power, we have also defined the purpose—to unite or reconcile *all* things; things in heaven and things on earth. This energy is not chaotic; that is the opposite of creativity—but moves toward a goal. We have given a simple name to this reconciling and unifying purpose. We have called it *love*.

From the highest to the lowest order of things, Christian theology asserts the presence and the power of this life force. The simplest molecule has a mission in mind. The very smallest fragments of the world seek each other so that existence might be continually possible. Sexuality is only one example of an irresistible attraction. All creation seeks out the rest of creation. In the "inanimate" world—as if there were things that existed but had no life—we call that seeking out "gravity." Without it everything would spin apart and there would be no universe. Yet the most simple flower on the most common bush defies gravity as it reaches for the sun. Thus a second evidence of a life force. Seeking out the other and reaching toward the sun are both elements of love.

We usually think of love only as a sentiment, which includes joy and misery. But consider love as this life force in which everything operates with a purpose. The purpose as well as the purposer we have called "God." God is at work, luring every part of creation to reach out to every other part—and simultaneously instilling in every molecule the desire to reach up, to break through the crust, to achieve some higher purpose.

While Christian theology affirms that there is a goal for history and for the natural order, we cannot define that goal with much specificity. It is shrouded in the Mystery. But if the dynamic force that impels everything is love, we can sense the broad outlines of where it is headed. We have identified that goal as the "reign of God." Its fullest explication comes to us through Jesus the Christ, who simultaneously called the creation, including us, to seek out one another, but also to reach for the higher and the nobler. He declared the wonder of a God, who while reaching out to us and to all creation, is powerfully moving with some nobler purpose toward an Omega point—a goal, a fulfillment in which the love, which is God, will be all in all.

Without specific knowledge, but with a trust in the power at work in history, and moved by love, Christian theology is profoundly hopeful. Hope is not the same as optimism. Optimism too easily rests in human achievement. Hope rests in the ultimate power of God. Optimism suggests that we will work things out. Hope affirms that it is all in the hands of God. Optimism assumes we are on a mechanical escalator and that every day in every way things are getting better and better. Hope affirms that in the darkest night and at the depths of the deepest tragedy God is still in charge. The central story of the Christian faith affirms that Jesus' death is not the end. God is still at work and the resurrection God's thunderous affirmation that the victory had already been won.

The Book of Revelation—A Call to Hope

While the Scriptures, Hebrew and Christian, are replete with testimonies to our hope, the book of Revelation has played a special role. It describes God's final victory, and is our handbook on hope. And yet it has been misunderstood and trivialized by those who have tried to distill from the complexity of its literary style specific allusions to political events in their own time.

Since history hasn't happened yet, and since God works with history, it violates both common sense and theological integrity to see specific current events prophesied in the book of Revelation or in other similar biblical materials. Almost since the day it was written, religious people have attempted to identify their own history in the poetry and imagery of the author. Peddlers of these prophetic misconceptions have in my lifetime seen in the book of Revelation: Germany, Japan, and Russia, Iran and Iraq as the demonic powers, and the United States—of course—as the new Jerusalem.

These days biblical fundamentalists, who consistently misuse these documents, have announced that the European Common Market, Social Security, and the most recent international tariff agreement are signs, all referred to in Revelation, that Jesus is about to return and the end of the world to follow.

This mauling results from a failure to pay attention to the historic context in which the book was written. What is the background and therefore the central theme and meaning of this marvelous hopeful testimony? One does not need to spend time in conjecture. The testimony of the text itself makes it clear.

A bishop, who cared for a number of churches in what we would now call southern Turkey, had been driven from his flock during a period of intense persecution, which took place about the end of the first Christian century. He had been subsequently exiled to a Mediterranean island. He knew that the Roman persecution and bloodshed afflicting his friends would only get worse. The churches under his care could not use the New Testament as their guide, since as yet there was no such authorized collection of books! With their leader gone and no authoritative documents to rely on they were in serious trouble—without moorings, direction, or leadership.

The bishop decides to keep in touch with his churches by letter. He sends one long message to all the churches, introducing it with very brief specific messages to each church. The body of the letter is written in a literary style common in that era. It is called an *apocalypse,* and was popular in the East. For those in the West, Rome for instance, it would appear to be an obscure poetic tale. Thousands of these apocalypses existed, and they all told a similar story:

Life is good but evil penetrates the world. Evil appears to be victorious. Indeed, the terror with which it afflicts the righteous is devastating. All seems to be lost, and there is nothing anyone can do. The good stand by and watch helplessly. Many die. God, however, counterattacks and there is a fierce battle in which good finally prevails. Those who die are honored. Those who survive inherit a beautiful new world.

There were variations, but that is essentially the message common to all apocalyptic literature.

This bishop probably had access to a library of apocalyptic books from which he borrowed, putting together his own version. The message to the faithful is simple: Hold on! Things are going to get bad, and after that they will get worse! Many of you will die. It will be a terrifying time, but God will finally prevail. The perfect world, which existed before evil invaded, would be fully restored.

Assume you were a member of one of those churches facing persecution. The times were treacherous. The terror was building in intensity. Would your pastor, who had been forced out of town, meet your needs by sending you a document describing what nations of Europe would do two thousand years in the future—even if he knew? That sort of communication would be useless. But the bishop is not talking about events far down the future. In the first sentence he tells his readers that he will be describing events that will "soon take place" (Revelation 1:1).

The book of Revelation gave hope to those caught in the jaws of the beast sitting on her seven hills, an obvious reference to Rome (Revelation 17:9). It also described the awesome and ultimate power of God, and that is its basic message. It is a book of hope, not only for those to whom it was originally written, but for anyone in distress.

After much wrangling, the church finally included it in the official list of books that could be read at worship. Yet it has led to so much confusion and drawn so many people off in exotic directions over the centuries that there are those still unconvinced it belongs in the Christian canon. Luther would have none of it, and others have held that it has generated more mischief than hope.

The Last Word

Christian theology affirms that while the future is open, it is not up for grabs. The closing chapters have not yet been written because the events have not yet occurred. But without knowing the text, we know the author whose life becomes the text. The fundamental authority and power in history is God, the active agent of all existence, a force that moves with power and purpose. God will win the inevitable victory. And this same God, in whose hands rests tomorrow, is alive and at work today. At every hour we can affirm that the victory has already been won.

Even so, we are part of the victory. Our lives, the life of the community of faith, indeed the whole cosmos is called to live and work together, standing on tiptoes, looking for God's final YES. The resurrection of Christ is, for us, the sign of this affirming confluence. If we understand the resurrection to be no more than a physical resuscitation in which God violated the laws of nature, we fail to recognize the impact of the event. There are many stories of heroes rising from the dead—others in the Bible. Here rather is the testimony that at the darkest moment God was at work. A God who keeps upsetting the natural law would create more problems than could be solved. We survive only as we trust the law of gravity—and other natural laws—to be dependable.

Our faith does not rest in a God who can do supernatural tricks, a Christian version of the genie in a bottle. God does not cause it to rain or stop raining for our benefit. But God is at work all the time opening up the future. God encounters us at the very edge of what is not yet. God is an infinitely rich world of possibilities ready to happen. The miracle takes place when we meet this God on the edge of what is not yet. A whole new epoch was spread before those who were witnesses to the purposeful power—we call it love—not even death could stop. It was true during the events surrounding Jesus' passion. It is true today. Everything that happens brings with it an infinite cluster of what is not yet. God is more than the first cause. God is the continual cause, the sum total of all that is potential. Our response is called faith, and it is that faith which moves mountains.

Centered on the resurrection of Jesus the Christ, and moving through evidence generated in the Great Conversation, we observe the penetration of the future into the present. God will not only triumph, God is triumphing now.

The creative energy, which we call love, is not just an attribute of God. God *is* love! It is what moves the world toward the ultimate victory, and will not wear out. Love is not just how we define where the world is headed, it is the process by which it is headed there. It can be counted on, now and in the future.

We, therefore, do not face enemies who will ultimately be victorious. Every enemy is already defeated. The powers, principalities and rulers of darkness have been disarmed. God has already triumphed over them. As God stood at the beginning of history as the source of creation, stands in the midst of history as its sustainer, so God will stand at the end of history as its consummator, liberator, and victor. Beyond the pious hope that someday God will win out, we live in the conviction that the victory has already been accomplished.

No matter the appearances, we no longer need to be taken in by those who are fixated on defeat and deceit, or by any philosophy that asserts that might makes right. Love makes right! And love has won, is winning and will win the final victory. Power with a purpose, the God who is able to do far more abundantly than all we ask or think; that is the heart of all theology.

From the assurance of God's final cosmic victory, in which all things are redeemed and reconciled, to the affirmation that this purposeful love cares for each one of us in life and in death, we affirm God's triumph. To know this God is to have eternal life. "To the only God our Savior, through Jesus Christ our Lord, be glory, majesty, power, and authority, before all time and now and forever. Amen" (Jude 25).

For Further Reading

Charles H. Bayer, *Hope for the Mainline Church* (St. Louis: CBP Press, 1991). A recent work by the present author that serves as a practical handbook for the recovery of strength by mainline Protestant congregations.

Robert McAfee Brown, *Liberation Theology: An Introductory Guide* (Louisville: Westminster/John Knox Press, 1993). A very readable introduction to one of the theological perspectives discussed in Chapter Ten.

John B. Cobb, Jr., *Becoming a Thinking Christian* (Nashville: Abingdon Press, 1993). A guidebook for laypeople on how to go about achieving a renewal of thinking, as a basis for church renewal.

John B. Cobb, Jr., *Lay Theology* (St. Louis: Chalice Press, 1994). Written by a major contemporary theologian who insists that the doing of theology properly belongs in the church.

Robert Mesle, *Process Theology: A Basic Introduction* (St. Louis: Chalice Press, 1993). A very readable introduction to the theological point of view that underlies the approach of this book.

David P. Polk, ed., *What's a Christian to Do?* and *Now What's a Christian to Do?* (St. Louis: Chalice Press, 1991, 1994). Each volume explores six tough issues facing Christians today in an innovative format that invites theological reflection in individual or group study.